Angel Numbers

Unlock the Secrets of Angels, Divine Messages, Numerology, Synchronicity, and Symbolism

Your Free Gift
(only available for a limited time)

Thanks for getting this book! If you want to learn more about various spirituality topics, then join Mari Silva's community and get a free guided meditation MP3 for awakening your third eye. This guided meditation mp3 is designed to open and strengthen ones third eye so you can experience a higher state of consciousness. Simply visit the link below the image to get started.

https://spiritualityspot.com/meditation

Table of Contents

Introduction

Have you ever noticed that the same angel numbers seem to pop up repeatedly and wondered what they meant? Angel numbers are ways through which divine entities try to communicate with humans and offer them support and guidance whenever needed. It's not a coincidence if your eyes repeatedly fall on 333, 444, or other repeated numerical sequences. Each sequence carries a unique meaning that offers insight into certain aspects of your life. Paying attention to angel numbers is a step towards personal growth and development.

In this book, you'll learn all about angel numbers, the secrets of angels, divine messages, numerology, synchronicity, and symbolism. It's an interesting yet informative read that explores the spiritual significance of angel numbers and how they serve as a self-exploratory development practice. It delves into the concept of angel numbers and uncovers the history and origins of this age-old divination technique.

By reading this book, you'll understand the role of various angelic and divine beings and how they communicate with humans through specific signs and symbols. You'll learn about the basics of numerology and the different numerology systems. In this chapter, you'll learn about the most common numerical sequences and their meanings. You'll also understand the role that one's intuition plays when interpreting these sequences.

The book explains how angel signs, like coincidences, bodily sensations, scents, objects, and unexpected occurrences, can manifest. It lists the symbols and sigils of various angels and offers several meditations and prayers that you can try out.

The book also illustrates the difference between the concepts of synchronicity, divine timing, and coincidence. You'll learn what synchronicity is and how it's relevant to today's spiritual practices. You'll understand the universal rules that govern and dictate divine timing and learn how to distinguish between synchronicities and coincidences.

In addition to angel numbers, sequences, and sigils, this guide also explores other angelic correspondences. You'll understand how angels are associated with things like days of the week, hours of the day, zodiac signs, colors, months, and gemstones. You'll find a list that covers the correspondences for the most popular angelic figures.

There's an entire chapter dedicated to the concept of the Law of Attraction that explains how it works and the main philosophical and religious principles on which it is based. You'll find out how angelic correspondences can be used in tandem with the Law of Attraction and learn about several practical exercises, such as meditations and visualization, which can help you put your knowledge into practice. These activities will guide you in activating the Law of Attraction for specific goals.

The book's last chapter serves as a mini directory of daily meditations with which you can practice enhancing your awareness, connect to the angelic realm, and open your third eye and crown chakras. You'll also find grounding techniques and exercises which help with energy cleansing, practices that aid in uncovering synchronicities in the past, and meditations on angel symbols and numbers.

Chapter 1: What Are Angel Numbers?

Do you ever experience a series of weird coincidences where you see certain number sequences everywhere you look? Maybe it's the number 1111 on a digital clock or 333 on license plates and bills. These occurrences may seem like coincidences initially, but when they become more frequent, they could be a sign from the angels. Many spiritual beliefs signal the existence of angel numbers - number sequences that hold spiritual value beyond their numeric meaning. Many people consider them a message from the divine, the universe, and angels. These numbers can appear on clocks, phone numbers, receipts, license plates, and even in dreams. People are divided between firmly believing in the existence of these numbers and being skeptical about the divine presence and messages from the universe. This chapter will be about the belief in angels and how they can communicate with you.

Angelic/Divine Beings

Even if you're not religious, you're probably familiar with angels. Maybe you know them from fiction, movies, or books. They are depicted as divine beings who have wings and special abilities. Angels have been revered in many religions and beliefs since ancient civilizations. And people have always been equally curious and fascinated with the concept of angels. From biblical stories to modern-day accounts, the mere concept of angels has captured the imagination of humans worldwide.

There are so many stories of angel sightings. Some people describe these interactions as a bright light or hearing a heavenly choir during near-death experiences. Others feel a presence over their shoulders looking out for them, offering them guidance and protection. For instance, have you ever had a near-accident experience where you maybe almost stepped in front of an oncoming car but somehow avoided the accident by a second? You never know; this might be the work of your guardian angel.

According to most spiritual traditions, angels are considered to be God's messengers and helpers. They're considered celestial beings of light and love, able to protect and comfort those in need. In some traditions, angels are believed to have individual responsibilities, like looking over humans, delivering God's messages, or overseeing elements or seasons. In Christianity, for instance, there are nine choirs of angels, with the highest rank being Seraphim and the lowest rank being mere angels. Each of these choirs has a specific role in serving God and humanity.

1. The Seraphim

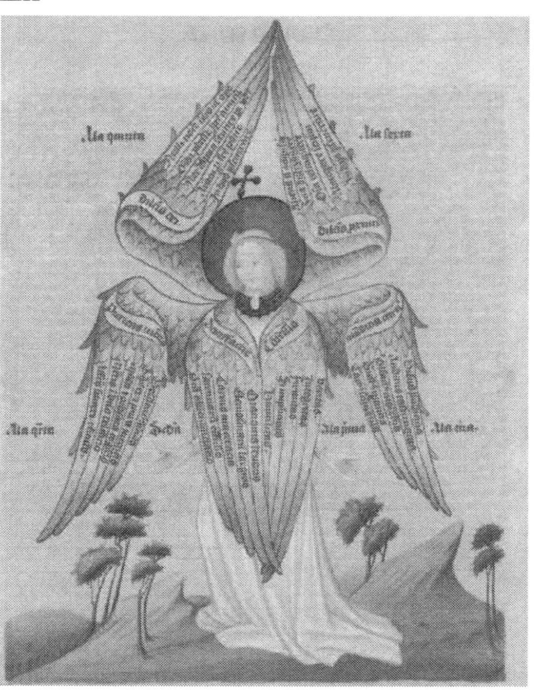

Seraphim are pure light or fire, reflecting their intense love for God.

https://picryl.com/media/postilla-in-prophetas-ubu-hs-252-f043v-moralisacio-seraph-3655d7

At the top of the hierarchy of angels are the Seraphim. They are considered pure light or fire; their name translates to "burning ones," reflecting their intense love and devotion to God. According to religious literature, they have six wings; two cover their faces, two cover their feet, and the remaining two are used to fly. These angels are the closest to the divine presence and most likely don't interact with humans.

2. The Cherubim

Next in the hierarchy are the Cherubim. They are believed to be the guardians of God's throne. They are often depicted as having four faces: a human, a lion, an ox, and an eagle, representing their diverse knowledge and wisdom. The Cherubim are known for their understanding of the mysteries of God and their role in protecting His divine presence.

3. The Thrones

The third choir of angels is the Thrones, believed to embody God's justice and authority. They are considered fiery wheels or chariots, which is a representation of their swift and powerful nature. The Thrones are responsible for upholding divine order and maintaining balance in the universe.

4. The Dominions

Next in the hierarchy are the Dominions, who are believed to be the guardians of the cosmos. They oversee the work of the lower ranks of angels and are depicted as holding scepters or orbs, symbolizing their authority and power. The Dominions make sure that the universe functions according to God's will.

5. The Virtues

The Virtues are known for their courage and strength, and they are responsible for maintaining the balance between the spiritual and physical worlds. They are seen as warriors in armor, wielding swords and shields and fighting for God's will. They keep the world in harmony and balance.

6. The Powers

The Powers are responsible for defending humanity against spiritual and physical harm. They are depicted wielding swords or shields, symbolizing their strength and protective nature. The Powers watch over the world and keep humans safe.

7. The Principalities

The Principalities are believed to be the guardians of nations and empires. They are responsible for maintaining order and harmony in the world, and they hold keys or scrolls, symbolizing their role as stewards of governance. The Principalities ensure that nations and empires operate according to God's plan.

8. The Archangels

The Archangels are known for their role as messengers of God, delivering vital messages to humanity. They are often associated with specific tasks, such as healing or protection, and they are responsible for carrying out God's will on Earth.

9. The Angels

Finally, at the lowest rank of the hierarchy are the Angels. They are responsible for carrying out the tasks assigned to them by the higher levels and are often depicted as messengers or helpers. Angels serve God and humanity in various ways, offering humans their love, protection, and guidance.

One common category of angels you might have heard about is the guardian angels. These angels are considered unique to every individual, assigned to every human at birth, and tasked with protecting them throughout life. They watch over you, protect you from harm, both physical and otherwise, and offer you comfort and guidance. They protect you from negative energies and prevent you from making bad decisions in life. Guardians are not limited to a single religion or belief and can be present with every individual, regardless of their belief. Even if you do not want to believe in the existence of actual angels, you could still consider the guidance that comes from angel numbers to be messages from the universe. These divine energies exist beyond the boundaries of space and time, watching over you and guiding you on your spiritual journey. So, while it may seem like a stretch to some people, when you start believing in this concept and manifesting divine guidance, you'll be surprised where this road ends up taking you.

Origins of Angel Numbers

The existence of angel numbers can be traced as far back as the Babylonians and Egyptians. They were of the view that numbers held mystical significance and that they could be used to communicate with the divine. Initially, the Babylonians developed a complicated numerology system related to astrology. They laid the foundation for the idea that each number had a unique vibration corresponding to a specific celestial body. That is when astrology was born, and people's birth dates and locations could provide valuable insight into their life.

On the other hand, the Egyptians believed that they were closely tied to religious beliefs. For instance, the number 7 was especially revered in ancient Egypt because it represented the seven pillars of wisdom and the seven gods of creation. They also believed that the number 42 was a representation of the path to eternal life. These ancient beliefs set the foundation for the connection between numerology and angel numbers.

Over time, this concept became more complex, with more research and religious connections being made to its existence. In particular, Christianity has a lot of references to special numbers and the meanings behind them. For instance, the number 3 is believed to represent the holy trinity, whereas the number 7 is believed to represent perfection or completion. This concept was developed even further during the Middle Ages when numerology was introduced to the world. Both scholars and philosophers were fascinated by the mystical aspects of numbers and their connection to the divine. They truly believed that numbers would help them uncover the universe's secrets.

One of the most famous works on numerology from that period is the "Liber Abaci," written by the Italian mathematician Leonardo Fibonacci in 1202. In it, Fibonacci introduced the concept of the Fibonacci sequence, a series of numbers where each one is the sum of the two preceding numbers. This sequence is found in nature and has been used in architecture, music, and art for centuries. Fibonacci also introduced the concept of Arabic numerals to Europe, revolutionizing mathematics and making calculations easier.

Angel Numbers as a Spiritual Practice

In recent years, the concept and practice of angel numbers have become a fully-fledged spiritual belief, with so many people regularly seeking guidance and insight from the angels. People who have experienced the sightings of angel numbers believe that the more faith you have, the clearer the messages will be. At first, you will surely be skeptical about the whole thing, but once you see it in action and actually make a good life decision following this advice, your belief will only get stronger. Much like tarot and astrology, interpreting angel numbers has become very popular, with more and more people being interested in learning more about it.

Let's consider an example to examine how exactly angel numbers work. Jake is going through a tough time in his life. He just lost his job and is struggling to find a new one. His financial situation has worsened by the day, and he feels like giving up entirely on the job search. One day, as he's walking down the street, he notices the number 888 appearing everywhere he looks. First, he sees it on a billboard ad, then he finds it on his grocery receipt, then a truck's license plate, and on and on. At first, he thinks it's just a coincidence, but after the sightings become frequent, Jake starts researching what this number means. That is when he comes across angel numbers and how they work. Already feeling lost and discouraged, he takes this as a sign that his financial situation would improve if he followed the advice associated with this angel number. Encouraged by this, he does exactly that and soon gets a job offer much better than he expected. This experience proved to be a learning moment for him, and his belief in angel numbers was reinforced by it.

This story offers a glimpse into the power and potential of angel numbers as a spiritual practice. Whether used to receive guidance during difficult times or as a daily practice for spiritual growth and exploration, the interpretation of angel numbers can offer individuals a powerful tool for connecting with the divine and finding guidance and support on their spiritual journey.

Places Where Angel Numbers Can Appear

Have you ever been driving down the road, and a series of numbers on a license plate caught your eye? Maybe you were at the grocery store, and the total on your receipt added up to a repeating sequence of numbers. These are just a couple of examples of how angel numbers can appear in the most unexpected places and how they can be easy to miss if we're not paying attention. Where else can you expect to find these angelic messages? The truth is, they can appear just about anywhere. Some people have reported seeing angel numbers on digital clocks, such as 11:11 or 3:33. Others have seen them on billboards, house numbers, or even in patterns of leaves or clouds. The possibilities are truly endless, but here are some of the most common places:

1. Digital Clocks and Watches

Digital clocks and watches are perhaps the most common place where people see angel numbers. It's not uncommon to glance at your phone, computer, or watch and see repeated numbers. Sometimes, the appearance of angel numbers on digital clocks and watches can be quite bizarre. One woman reported that every time she checked the time on her digital watch, the display showed the number 444. Even when she changed the battery, the watch continued to show 444.

2. License Plates

License plates can be another unexpected location to find angel numbers. Whether driving to work, running errands, or simply taking a stroll around the block, keep an eye out for license plates with repeating or sequential numbers. It may seem like a coincidence, but some people believe that seeing certain numbers on a license plate is a sign from their guardian angels. For example, let's say you've been contemplating a big life decision and keep seeing the number 888 on license plates. You might interpret this as a message from your angels that you're on the right path and that your decision will bring abundance and prosperity into your life.

3. Street Addresses and House Numbers

Another common way people encounter angel numbers is street addresses and house numbers. This is because the numbers used in these addresses are often chosen randomly, yet they can still hold significant meanings for those living there. For example, let's say you're house hunting and come across a property with the address 777. To some, this may simply seem like a nice, easy-to-remember number. But to those who believe in the power of angel numbers, the triple sevens could represent a message from the divine realm. In numerology, 777 is often associated with spiritual awakening, inner wisdom, and good fortune.

4. Receipts

Receipts are a surprising yet common place where people have reported seeing angel numbers. When you get a receipt after a purchase, it's easy to quickly glance at it before throwing it away. However, if you're open to the idea of angel numbers, you might be surprised to see them appear on your receipt. For example, imagine you went to the grocery store and bought a few items for a total of $22.22. You might think nothing of it at first, but if you're paying attention, you'll realize this is a powerful message from your angels. The number 22 is associated with balance and harmony, while the repeated appearance of the number 2 amplifies its significance. This could be a message to focus on finding balance in your life or that everything is working together for your highest good.

5. Phone Numbers

Phone numbers are another place where people may encounter angel numbers. You might receive a call from a number that ends in 1111 or 2222. These repeating digits could be a sign that you should pay attention to the caller's message. Some people even choose phone numbers that contain angel numbers as a way to bring positive energy into their lives. For instance, a person might intentionally choose a phone number that ends in 8888 because they believe it will bring them good luck. In some instances, people have even reported receiving phone calls from numbers that don't seem to exist. One woman repeatedly received calls from a number that ended in 1111. However, she discovered it wasn't a valid number when she tried calling back.

6. Books or Other Printed Materials

Books and other printed materials can also contain hidden messages in the form of angel numbers. For example, imagine you are reading a novel and notice that the page number is 222. This could be interpreted as a sign that the plot is about to take a significant turn or that the character is about to experience a moment of transformation. Similarly, textbooks and self-help books may have certain sections or chapters that are particularly important for the reader to pay attention to. These sections may be marked by the appearance of angel numbers, such as 111 or 555. It's not just the material's content that can contain angel numbers but also anything pertaining to the publication. For example, a book published on 11/11 at 11:11 could hold special significance for the reader.

7. Social Media

In today's digital age, social media has become an integral part of our lives, and it's not surprising that angel numbers can appear there too. Many have reported seeing them while scrolling through Instagram, Facebook, or Twitter. For instance, someone might come across a post with 111 likes or a tweet retweeted 444 times. Others might see the numbers 222 or 555 as the time stamp on a message or notification. Some might even notice a specific number sequence in the follower count of their favorite influencer or brand.

8. Billboards or Advertisements

Ads and billboards can be another interesting place to spot angel numbers. You might notice a billboard while driving or walking down the street. As you look at it, you notice that the phone number or website address contains the sequence of numbers you have seen lately. It could be a combination of 111, 222, or any other number sequence. For example, you might see an ad for a local business with a phone number ending in 333 or a billboard with a website address that includes 444. These numbers can be interpreted as a message from angels urging you to notice the business or its products and services.

Recognizing Angel Numbers

Recognizing angel numbers is the first step in interpreting their message. These numbers may appear to you in many different forms and combinations, and it's essential to be aware of them. Here are some tips to help you recognize and understand angel numbers:

1. **Pay Attention to Repetition:** One of the most common ways in which angel numbers appear is through repetition. If you keep seeing the number 1111 or 2222, it's a clear sign that the angels are trying to communicate with you. Take note of any number sequences that keep appearing to you.
2. **Look for Unusual Number Sequences**: Angel numbers can appear in various number sequences, including triple digits, quadruple digits, or even mixed numbers. Be aware of any number combinations that catch your attention or seem out of the ordinary.
3. **Notice Your Intuition:** Often, your intuition can guide you to recognize angel numbers. If a particular number sequence catches your attention, pay attention to how you feel when you see it. Do you get a feeling of joy or peace? Do you feel like it's a sign from the universe?
4. **Stay Open to Signs:** Angel numbers can appear in many ways, including through dreams, music, and even our daily routines. Keep an open mind and trust that the angels will reach out in a way that is meant for you.

5. **Use Your Inner Guidance:** Ultimately, interpreting angel numbers is a personal journey, and you should trust your intuition and inner guidance. Look within yourself for answers, and let your intuition guide you toward understanding the messages the angels send you.

Angel numbers can be pretty powerful if you believe in them and take the advice they're trying to convey. It doesn't matter if you believe in divine beings or not; you can simply consider angel numbers to be messages from the universe. After all, there's little doubt that there's some universal mystical energy around us, say *karmic energy*, or whatever belief you find reasonable. There's something so undeniably magical about the appearance of certain numbers so frequently that it can't possibly be a simple coincidence. So, the next time you see a repeated sequence, pay attention to it and discover what it means; you never know where it may lead.

Chapter 2: Numerology 101

The concept of angel numbers wasn't the first of its kind. In fact, it all started when philosophers and theorists started to pay attention to the special qualities of numbers. This explains how the concept of numerology - the belief that numbers hold significant meaning - came about; if studied enough, they can reveal the mysteries of the universe. To learn why angel numbers hold such importance, you must first learn about numerology and its associated theories. Essentially, numerology sets the foundation for interpreting the symbolism and unique messages behind angel numbers. Initially, numerology was nothing more than a mathematician pondering the hidden messages behind numbers. It has deep roots in history, with concepts from Greece, Egypt, and China.

This chapter will provide you with a brief introduction to numerology, how it originated, and the different types of numerology systems that have been developed since. Once you've fully grasped numerology, you can move on to understanding and interpreting angel numbers. Unlike other numerology practices focusing on birth information and astrological signs, angel number sequences can appear to anyone at any time.

What Is Numerology?

The universe has a language of its own, one that can speak to you through a series of numbers, symbols, and energies. The communication system consisting of numbers is known as numerology, and it essentially holds the key to unlocking the secrets of the world around you. At its core, numerology studies the link between numbers and their corresponding events. It's a language with perfect synchrony, where everything from your life's patterns to your name's vibrations holds significance. You can find your place in the universe by uncovering the numerical value of words, names, and symbols. That is what numerology is all about. Every person is born with a soul, an eternal and non-physical essence that is imbued with a unique name and energetic symbolism.

The Origins of Numerology

The study of numerology is a tapestry woven with threads of ancient wisdom and timeless insight. Its roots run deep, extending far beyond the introduction of its name and into the very fabric of the universe. While numerology is considered to be a science by most people, it's actually a belief system that has a rich history spanning the entirety of human existence. From the first moment humans started to recognize the powers of numerals and mathematics, the theories and practices of numerology were already likely in motion. Among the first to utilize this concept were the ancient Egyptians. At the time, they weren't aware that the spiritual system they were practicing would be developed into the vast field of numerology. Pythagoras, the great mathematician and theorist, is considered the pioneer of numerology.

The theories by Pythagoras, especially those about numbers and music notes, were considered groundbreaking and essentially led to the development of a direct relationship between the two subjects. Through his mathematical knowledge, Pythagoras could identify people's personality traits based on their birth dates and corresponding vibrational notes. He was a firm believer in the power of numbers and suggested that everything in the universe could be explained by numbers. The principles given by him are still used in modern numerology, which is also known as the Pythagorean Number System.

Pythagoras is considered to be the pioneer of Numerology.

The word "numerology" was only introduced in 1907, but the concept and importance of numbers have been present in all religions and belief systems way before that. Birthdays, anniversaries, and other significant dates hold deep meaning and value for most individuals.

Pythagoras' Teachings on Numerology

While Pythagoras is commonly known for his discovery of the Pythagorean theorem, with which you're probably familiar from high-school mathematics, his contributions to numerology are equally significant. In fact, many consider him to be the inventor of Western numerology. According to Aristotle, Pythagoreans held a mystical reverence for mathematics and believed that all things in the universe were composed of numbers. They saw them not only as means of quantifying the world around them but also as a powerful tool for unlocking deeper truths about the nature of existence. For the

Pythagoreans, the study of numerology was not simply an intellectual pursuit but a deeply spiritual one. They believed that by understanding the vibrational energies of numbers, they could gain insight into the hidden forces that govern the universe and that this knowledge could be used to achieve a greater understanding of the self and the world around them.

One of the most important teachings of Pythagoras included the concept of the Divine Triangle, a sacred symbol that would become a cornerstone of numerology. At the heart of the Divine Triangle is the number 3, representing the three aspects of the universe: the physical, the intellectual, and the spiritual. The triangle itself symbolizes harmony and balance, with each of its sides and angles representing different aspects of life. The triangle's base represents the physical world, with its material possessions and earthly pleasures. The left side represents the intellectual world, where your thoughts and ideas take shape. The right side represents the spiritual world, where you connect with your higher self and the divine. Other theories from Pythagoras' teachings will be explained in the Pythagoras' numerology section.

Different Numerology Systems

Numerology is a vast belief system that isn't limited to a single interpretation. In fact, there are multiple types of numerology systems based on how they use numeric values and interpretations to define various aspects of the universe or the individuals residing in said universe. Some of the most well-known numerology systems include:

1. Chaldean Numerology

This ancient numerology system has its roots in Babylonia. It consists of complex mathematical calculations and a unique perspective. Unlike Pythagorean numerology, this system assigns numbers to the vibrations produced by letters instead of simply corresponding to them. According to the teachings of this system, numbers hold a lot more value than just their numeric values. They can correspond to different planets, heavenly bodies, and universal energies associated with life's creation. The Chaldean numerology practitioners consider this practice a spiritual and mystical tool.

Pythagorean numerology, as opposed to Chaldean numerology, uses a more straightforward method of allocating numbers to letters based on where they are located in the alphabet. While the Pythagorean approach may be more straightforward, some numerology practitioners consider Chaldean numerology to be slightly more accurate. Chaldean numerology is distinctive in that it gives letter values of 1 through 8 while reserving the number 9 as "holy." However, if the sum of a name's numerical values is 9, it is retained. Additionally, Chaldean numerology requires practitioners to use the name by which a person is most commonly known rather than their full birth name.

For instance, if the actor Michael Douglas used Chaldean numerology, he would be referred to as "Michael Douglas" instead of "Michael Kirk Douglas," his full birth name.

2. Indian Numerology

Indian numerology, also known as Vedic numerology, is a system of mystical interpretation that assigns numerical values to the letters of the Sanskrit alphabet. This system has been based on the belief that each letter in the Sanskrit alphabet has a unique vibrational energy that can provide deep insights into the spiritual realm and the mysteries of life. In Indian numerology, each letter is assigned a numerical value, ranging from 1 to 9. These numerical values are then used to calculate various aspects of a person's life, such as their personality traits, strengths, weaknesses, and life path. The calculations are usually based on a person's name and date of birth.

One of the key principles of Indian numerology is the idea of karma or the belief that a person's actions in this life are determined by their past lives. You've probably come across the word karmic energy before. According to this principle, a person's name and birth date are not arbitrary or random. Instead, they are calculated by their past karma and the lessons they need to learn in this lifetime. Indian numerology also includes the use of various numerical combinations and patterns, such as the use of repeating numbers, double numbers, and triple numbers. These patterns are believed to hold special significance and can provide insights into a person's spiritual path and destiny.

3. Kabbalistic Numerology

Kabbalistic numerology, or *Hebrew numerology*, provides the mystical interpretation that assigns numerical values to Hebrew letters and words. This system, again centering on corresponding letters and numbers, is based on the belief that every letter in the Hebrew alphabet has a unique vibrational energy and that these energies can be used to gain insights into the universe's secrets. In Kabbalistic numerology, each

Hebrew letter is assigned a numerical value, known as its gematria. The gematria of a word or phrase is calculated by adding up the numerical values of its constituent letters. For example, the word "chai" (meaning "life" in Hebrew) has a gematria of 18 because the letters Chet and Yud add up to 18.

Kabbalistic numerology also includes various numerical combinations and patterns, such as the number 72, which is believed to represent the 72 names of God. The practice of combining letters and numbers in this way is known as notarikon. Another aspect of Kabbalistic numerology is the Tree of Life, a symbolic diagram representing the divine flow of energy through the universe. Each of the ten sefirot (or spheres) on the Tree of Life is associated with a specific numerical value and represents a different aspect of divine energy.

Kabbalistic numerology is used more for divination and spiritual direction than anything else. This system is based more on spiritual guidance than numeric logic. In fact, just by looking at the gematria of your name or other significant words and phrases, you can gain helpful insights into your personality. Kabbalistic numerology is also used in the study of the Torah and other Hebrew texts, where numerical patterns and symbolism are believed to hold deep spiritual significance.

4. Chinese Numerology

Chinese numerology has been utilized for over 4,000 years, and it differs significantly from other numerological systems in that the Chinese believe that numbers are either naturally lucky or unlucky. In Eastern culture, luck plays a big role and is linked to the idea of fate. Chinese numerology places a lot of emphasis on a number's sound because they think certain sounds can bring good or bad luck. For instance, the Chinese word for "one" sounds similar to the English word "honor," signifying a person's capacity to overcome obstacles to achieve greater goals. In contrast, the term "four" has the same sound as "death," making the number 4 a bad omen that should be avoided.

Chinese people also believe that there are magical connections in numerical combinations. They contend that there is a link between the 12 rivers that flow in the direction of the Central Kingdom and the 12 blood and air veins that go throughout the body. Acupuncture targets 365 different body parts, corresponding to 365 days of the year.

The Lo Shu Square is the easiest way to use Chinese numerology. This method is based on a rumor that Emperor Yu saw a tortoise with nine perfect squares on its shell near the banks of the Luo River. The original Lo Shu Square is occasionally called the "Magic Square" because, when the numbers are summed up horizontally, vertically, or diagonally, they equal 15. The Lo Shu Square has nine cells, three rows, and three columns. Even numbers go in the corners, with the odd numbers forming a cross in the middle of the vertical and horizontal rows.

Recently, a modernized replica of Lo Shu Square has been created to teach Westerners Chinese numerology. The Hidden Cross, an upgraded form, uses fewer intricate calculations and does not require lunar years. The rows of the Hidden Cross are numbered from 1 to 9, and they are organized from top to bottom as follows: 3-6-9, 2-5-8, and 1-4-7. Understanding the meaning of the squares is necessary to interpret the outcome. The bottom row represents reality, the middle row represents feelings, and the top row represents ideas. From left to right, the columns stand for thinking, volition, and action, respectively.

5. Pythagoras Numerology

Pythagorean numerology is rooted in the work of the Greek mathematician Pythagoras, who believed that numbers were the universe's fundamental building blocks. This ancient practice views numbers as having mystical properties that can reveal much about a person and the world around them. Pythagoras believed that every object has a vibration, and numbers serve as a measure of that energy. The numbers 1 through 9 represent the nine stages of human life, with each number carrying its own symbolic meaning.

Pythagorean numerology has advanced into a complex system that examines a person's complete birth name and date of birth to give insights into their personality traits, motivations, inherent skills, and more. It can also provide valuable guidance on life patterns, timing, and decision-making. Pythagorean numerology has formed the spiritual basis for many secret societies and continues to be used as a tool for personal growth and self-discovery.

How Does It Work?

Modern numerology analyzes a person's full birth name and date to gain insight into their personality traits, strengths, weaknesses, and life patterns. It is based on the Pythagorean system of numerology, which assigns numerical values to letters in the alphabet and uses those values to calculate a person's core numbers. Here are the steps to practice modern numerology:

- In modern numerology, each letter is assigned a numerical value (between 1 and 9) based on its position in the alphabet. For example, A is assigned 1, B is assigned 2, C is assigned 3, and so on.
- Once you assign a numerical value to each letter in your full birth name, add all the values to get your Expression Number. Your Expression Number represents your natural talents, abilities, and tendencies.
- If your Expression Number is a double-digit number, reduce it to a single digit by adding the two digits together. For example, if your Expression Number is 34, add 3 + 4 = 7. Your reduced Expression Number is 7.
- Your Life Path Number is calculated using your date of birth. First, add your birth's day, month, and year together. Then, add the individual digits in the result to get a single-digit number. For example, if you were born on January 1, 1990, you would add 1 + 1 + 1 + 9 + 9 + 0 = 21. Then, you would add 2 + 1 = 3. Your Life Path Number is 3.
- Your Expression Number and Life Path Number represent your core numbers in modern numerology. These numbers can provide insight into your personality traits, strengths, weaknesses, and life patterns. Many online resources can help you interpret your core numbers.

Once you have calculated and interpreted your core numbers, you can use numerology to gain guidance in various areas of your life, like career, relationships, and personal growth. For example, you can use your core numbers to identify your strengths and weaknesses and to make decisions that align with your natural tendencies and desires.

Numerology and Angel Numbers

Numerology and angel numbers are closely connected, as both are based on the concept that numbers carry spiritual energy and can be used to communicate messages from the divine realm. Numerology provides a framework for understanding the meaning behind these angel numbers. They are unique in the sense that they are believed to be direct messages from the divine realm, whereas other esoteric practices in numerology focus more on using numbers to gain insight into a person's personality, life path, and future events. Angel numbers are not meant to provide personal readings or predictions. Rather, they are seen as guidance and support from the spiritual realm. Another difference is that angel numbers are often repetitive sequences of numbers, while other numerology systems may focus on individual numbers or combinations of numbers. For example, Pythagorean numerology assigns meanings to each number from 1 to 9, as well as to double-digit numbers and certain number combinations.

On the other hand, there are various similarities between angel numbers and other forms of numerology. For example, both angel numbers and Pythagorean numerology believe that each number has a unique vibrational energy that can influence our lives. Just as Pythagorean numerology assigns meaning to specific numbers based on their vibrational energy, angel numbers also have specific meanings based on the vibrational energy they carry. Similarly, in Kabbalistic numerology, each letter of the Hebrew alphabet is assigned a numerical value, and words and phrases can be analyzed based on their numerical value. This practice is similar to the interpretation of angel numbers, as both involve analyzing numerical patterns and sequences to gain insight and guidance.

Numerology Exercise

To better understand how the practice of numerology works, there's no better way than to practice it yourself. So, try out this personality analysis exercise to explore your inner self using numerology concepts. Follow these steps:

Step 1: Determine Your Life Path Number

The first step is to calculate your Life Path Number. This is done by adding up all the digits in your birth date and reducing it to a single digit. For example, if you were born on December 25, 1990, you would add 1+2+2+5+1+9+9+0 = 29. Then add 2+9=11. Finally, reduce 11 to a single digit by adding 1+1=2. Therefore, your Life Path Number would be 2.

Step 2: Understand Your Life Path Number

Each Life Path Number has a unique personality profile. For instance, Life Path Number 1 is known for being independent, driven, and ambitious, while Life Path Number 2 is known for being sensitive, intuitive, and nurturing. You can find a detailed description of each Life

Path Number's personality traits online or in numerology books.

Step 3: Calculate Your Expression Number

Your Expression Number is derived from your full name. To calculate it, assign a numerical value to each letter in your name using the chart below, then add up the numbers and reduce them to a single digit.

1 2 3 4 5 6 7 8 9

A B C D E F G H I

J K L M N O P Q R

S T U V W X Y Z

For example, if your name is John Doe, you would add 1+6+5+5+4+6+5 = 32. Then add 3+2 = 5. Therefore, your Expression Number would be 5.

Step 4: Understand Your Expression Number

Just like Life Path Numbers, Expression Numbers have unique characteristics. For example, Expression Number 1 is known for being independent, confident, and innovative, while Expression Number 5 is known for being adaptable, versatile, and adventurous. You can find a detailed description of each Expression Number's personality traits online or in numerology books.

Step 5: Interpret Your numbers

Now that you have your Life Path and Expression Numbers, it's time to interpret them. You can use numerology books and websites or consult a numerology expert to better understand your numbers. You can also use your intuition and reflect on your own experiences to connect with the meanings of your numbers.

Numerology isn't just a belief system. It is a comprehensive spiritual guideline for anyone looking to the universe for guidance. By understanding numerology, you can learn how numbers' symbolic meanings relate to your life. Angel numbers are a specific subset of numerology, and by learning the basics of numerology, you can begin to recognize the significance of these angel numbers and interpret their messages. So, essentially, learning everything you can about numerology is the first step in unlocking the secrets of angel numbers and connecting with the spiritual realm.

Chapter 3: Angel Numbers Interpreted

You likely came across angel numbers at some point and felt that the universe was trying to tell you something. Maybe a number combination kept popping up repeatedly in your life. You will know for sure if you're dealing with angel numbers when the appearance of these numbers starts becoming repetitive and doesn't feel like just a coincidence anymore. Maybe you looked up the meaning of the number combination you kept seeing and came up with an interpretation. But stop right there. Interpreting angel numbers isn't as simple as looking up the meaning of a word you found difficult. Interpreting these divine messages is an art form that needs a delicate balance of intuition and knowledge.

Each angel number has a deep meaning that you need to identify.

https://www.publicdomainpictures.net/en/view-image.php?image=339272&picture=numbers-and-digits

Sure, you can look up the meanings of the different numbers and their combinations, but that's just scratching the surface of the deep, deep rabbit hole that is angel numbers. Learning the different meanings of angel number combinations is just the tip of the iceberg, and only when you go beyond this will you fully interpret what they are exactly trying to tell you. The real magic starts happening when you interpret these numbers based on your unique perspective and experiences. Your situation, the context behind your dilemma, and your particular position about a matter all play into the final interpretation of your divine message. This chapter is about helping you learn the art of interpreting angel numbers while considering the factors mentioned above. But first, you should understand the basic meanings of the most commonly seen sequences. Let's start!

1 - Unity

Number one is often seen as the symbol of unity and wholeness. In fact, it has a lot of spiritual significance and is usually taken as a good sign. It's considered the beginning of all things or the starting point from where things emerge. According to many angel number interpretation guides, repeating 1s is representative of divine support. It symbolizes a new phase of self-actualization or the chance for a new beginning. Consider it an opportunity if you encounter this number as an angel number, whether repeated twice, thrice, or four times. It means the energy around you is very conducive and perfect for taking healthy steps forward. Consider this a green light from the universe, and either make a wish, take a risk, plant a seed, set an intention, or shift a pattern. Seeing this pattern should signal that you have your angels' support and that the present is dynamically connected to the future.

For instance, consider a woman named Alice. She has been in a long-term relationship with her partner Bob. Lately, she's been feeling somewhat unsure about their future and wondering if she should continue or move on. Imagine she has been encountering the number sequence 1111 everywhere she goes. It's on license plates, the digital clock, and even her grocery receipt. In her case, this sequence suggests that she should move forward with her relationship. Maybe she needs to shift a pattern or set an intention for the relationship to move to the next step. As another example, consider John, an entrepreneur planning to start a new business. While this is his dream, there are a lot of setbacks and demotivating people all around him who make him doubt if this is the right decision. This is when the angel number sequence 111 starts appearing to him everywhere. In his case, the angel numbers tell him to follow through on his plans.

2 - Finding Balance

In many cultures, the number two is seen as a sign of duality, balance, diplomacy, and harmony. The idea of duality is why 2 is seen as a balanced number. It reflects the balance between opposing forces. Take male and female, yin and yang, light and dark, all opposite pairs associated with the number 2. As an angel number, when it appears in a set of 2, 3, or 4, it could indicate that you're on the right path in an area of your life. It's a confirmation from the angels that you're headed in the right direction and should keep moving forward. Although you might not see results right then, consider this the groundwork you're laying. On the other hand, the appearance of this number could also signal a harmonious partnership, whether romantic, platonic, or professional. So, you should open yourself up to camaraderie, love, and trust whenever you see this angel number.

3 - Creativity and Artistic Expression

The number three indicates believing in yourself, your talents, wisdom, and creativity. Why is this number associated with creativity? Because it's often connected to the three Muses in Greek mythology. These deities were said to inspire art and creativity. This number suggests that you stand your ground and be clear about what you want in life. Apply your unique talents in whatever situation you're in, and you'll be able to get through. The presence of this number, whether in a set of 2, 3, 4, or within a pattern, signifies that you should lean into your special abilities and innate gifts to navigate your circumstances. In response, you'll get all the opportunities and resources needed to move forward.

For instance, assume you're having a tough time in your career. Maybe you've been applying to different jobs only to be rejected or ignored time and time again. Maybe you're starting to feel useless. Now, imagine you start to see the number 333 everywhere. You see it on your alarm clock and on your phone. In this case, the angels are guiding you toward success. This sequence reminds you to keep trying and to apply your unique abilities to your struggles to get successful.

4 - Stability and Structure

As an angel number, it signifies that you should ground yourself or are currently in the process of doing so. After accomplishing this, you may create a long-lasting infrastructure. This might apply to any situation, including a marriage, a home, or a company. If you have the angel number 4, don't hesitate to ask for assistance, especially if you're working on a long-term project that can't be finished independently. This will also assist in building a foundation of trust that will enable you to achieve greater success. Another meaning of 4 as an angel number, especially when it appears as 444, is that angels support you. People frequently see this sequence when they feel low and need some support.

5 - Freedom and Adventure

Five is often associated with the five elements of the universe: air, fire, water, earth, and spirit. It symbolizes the infinite possibilities that come with the combination of the five elements. You could also consider it a symbol of personal freedom and independence. When this number appears as an angel number sequence, it signals a future transformation or transition. Some major changes could be on the horizon, and instead of shying away from the dramatic changes you're going to go through, you should try to embrace the chaos if you have been feeling stuck, stifled, or experiencing a block. Seeing this sequence will shift the scales in your favor. Although, at the moment, it may seem like no changes are taking place within your life, these transformations are most definitely occurring behind the scenes. You might even feel like you have an invisible driving force that's pushing you toward these changes. Seeing a 555 pattern could also signify that you're not alone in whatever change you're going through. This pattern should remind you that, ultimately, you will get through whatever you're facing and come out the other side stronger.

Consider this example, Samantha is a single mother who has been feeling stuck in her dead-end job for years. She's been struggling to make ends meet and provide for her child. One day, she notices the number 555 repeatedly appearing on her clock, phone, and even on her social media feeds. Here, the sequence tells her that transformation and change are coming soon. Motivated by this, she takes it as a sign to take a leap of faith and pursue her dream of starting her own business. With the angels' guidance and her own abilities, she succeeds in achieving her goals.

6 - Unconditional Love

You've probably heard the misconceptions about the number six being associated with the Devil or other evil figures. However, as an angel number, sequence 666 signifies that the angels are supportive and empathetic with your situation. In fact, the number 6 is representative of beauty, balance, and grounding. Its energy is steady and nurturing. For that reason, this angel number should bring you feelings of comfort and relief. If you see it, remember to treat yourself kindly, compassionately, and with understanding. This sequence is also meant to remind you that although things didn't go according to how you planned, with the guidance of angel numbers and divine support, things will work out just fine in the end. You may also see this number if you're trying to bring peace, balance, and stability to an area in your life, whether it's your career, family, or finances. This number also encourages you to give yourself a break and stop working too hard. It could also signal that you need to let go of things that aren't serving you and may be dragging you down.

7 - Trusting Intuition and Spirituality

Everyone knows seven is a lucky number, especially when it appears as an angel number. It is also often connected with your spirituality and might appear when you focus on it or incorporate new practices into your life. Consequently, this number is related to pure divine guidance. It's all about serving the world and honoring the spiritual concept that binds you to the world. When you see this number repeatedly, it can be a sign that you are growing spiritually. It conveys that you should stay on this path. Seeing this number sequence could also be a sign that you may come into good fortune in the future, particularly financially.

8 - Abundance and Manifestation

The number eight is considered to be one of the most divine numbers. It's said to be even luckier than the number seven, especially regarding the financial aspect. Eight is also known as the angel number of abundance, which signals that the universe is going to send you more in terms of career, romance, or health. If you have an abundance of anything in your life, like money, love, or time, spread it around, and you'll likely be rewarded with even more. For people who have a belief in the afterlife, this angel number signals that their loved ones are watching over them and supporting them.

9 - Endings and New Beginnings

Nine is the final digit in numerology and is therefore considered to symbolize the end of a chapter in your life. Life is cyclical, and all things must come to an end. If you witness nine as an angel number sequence, it might mean that a meaningful journey is ending. This could include both good and bad experiences. This number appears to remind you that you should let go of things that have run their course instead of clinging to them. Although it might be difficult initially, you'll soon find out why ending things was important. If you see this angel number, know that this would be a great time to step out of your comfort zone, explore new opportunities, and expand your horizons.

Mirror Numbers

Mirror numbers can be called the Yin and Yang of numerology because they represent the ultimate balance and symmetry between two opposite sides. But what exactly are they? Mirror numbers are number sequences of 3 or 4 numerals that are the same when read backward. For instance, 121, 353, 1001, 1551, etc. See how the sequence remains the same even backward? Why are mirror numbers important? They are a special kind of angel number sequence that symbolizes a connection between the spiritual and physical worlds. They are a reminder that everything is connected and you're a reflection of the world around you.

To interpret mirror numbers, you should refer to the meanings of each one and then come up with a combined interpretation for the sequence. For instance, if you see the number sequence 1001 popping up everywhere, consider the meanings of 1 and 0. The number 1 reflects a chance for new beginnings, while the zero represents wholeness and spirituality. So, maybe this number sequence means that you've been given a new opportunity that you're pursuing by letting your spirituality guide you. Some common mirror number sequences include:

- **01:10 -** this sequence suggests you have a blank page for new beginnings, love, or more. You have the chance to start over in an area of your life.

- **02:20** - this sequence points towards a good career or lucrative opportunity in the future.
- **05:50** - this particular mirror number sequence represents adventure.
- **10:01** - this is one of the most magical mirror numbers. If you come across this, make a wish.
- **12:21** - this sequence suggests that you should be more careful and conscious of your actions.
- **13:31** - this particular sequence is a reminder that you should be aware of the opportunities that are all around you.
- **14:41** - this powerful mirror number signals incoming love and passion.
- **15:51** - this sequence suggests that you are at the right place and that you should listen to your intuition and move forward.

Personal Interpretation

Why is personal interpretation so important when it comes to angel numbers? Well, think of it this way: Angel numbers are like snowflakes, and no two interpretations can be exactly alike. How so? The context of the situation matters a lot, and so does the timing of the sighting, the person's mood, and what thoughts are on their mind.

Consider two people who have been seeing the number sequence 444 for a few days in a row. Having just lost his job, the first person is in a state of worry and despair and is feeling hopeless. For this person, the appearance of the number 4 can be a reminder that they will soon achieve stability in their life. It could also be a sign that angels are watching over this person, giving them hope and comfort.

The second person keeps seeing the same number while on vacation in a tropical paradise. They feel relaxed and carefree, so this angel number sequence gently reminds them to stay grounded and focused. In this context, the appearance of the number 4 is a comforting affirmation that they're exactly where they're supposed to be.

The interpretation process for the same sequence can vary. Since this is a deeply personal process, everyone has different interpretations.

Tips for Interpreting Angel Numbers

So, how should you go about interpreting an angel number you've been seeing everywhere? There are some steps you can take to interpret the divine message you're being sent.

1. Focus on Your Thoughts

Before you can move on to discover the meanings of the numbers that appear to you, you need to consider your thoughts first. The meanings of angel number sequences can seem generic and even vague if you don't consider your thoughts and feelings. So, take a moment to reflect on your emotions and what you're thinking. What thoughts are stressing you out, or which emotions have you been feeling the most recently? These are all questions you should ask yourself before you jump into interpreting the meanings of numbers.

2. Consider the Context

The context of a situation is what shapes your interpretation. Suppose you don't consider the situation you're in when you see angel numbers. In that case, the interpretation will be incomplete and pretty much useless. Consider the context, circumstances, and situation you're dealing with. Maybe you're happy with a new relationship or confused about starting one. Maybe you're starting a new project but have doubts about it. Whatever the situation, the angel numbers should guide you through them, and you should therefore consider the link between the numbers and your situation.

3. Consider Combinations

Angel number sequences can appear in double, triple, and four-digit sets. How do their meanings differ? What's the difference between 333 and 3333? Does the meaning change or simply get amplified? Triple digits are power numbers, whereas four digits represent enlightenment and the need for trust. Yes, four-digit sets are more powerful than triple-digit sequences. So, consider this factor before you interpret the meanings of these sequences. You may also encounter a mirror number or number sequences like 2323. This is where you'll have to combine the meanings as discussed previously.

4. Keep a Journal

One of the best ways to interpret angel number sequences is by keeping a journal. Note down all the considerations and answers you come up with. Track any patterns or themes that are consistent with the angel numbers you're seeing. For instance, if you notice you keep seeing angel numbers related to creativity, note down any creative endeavors you're involved in. Write down the context, your thoughts, and anything else you feel is relevant.

5. Trust Your Intuition

Last but not least, trust your gut. Your intuition is a powerful tool, especially when it comes to interpreting angel numbers. If a number sequence speaks to you, consider its meaning and your particular situation. Then, come up with an interpretation that your intuition points towards, even if it doesn't seem like a great idea at the moment.

Interpretation is all about what's inside you, your guiding light, thoughts, feelings, and intuition. Your intuition should play a major role in what your interpretation turns out to be. As Paul Coelho said, "Intuition is really a sudden immersion of the soul into the universal current of life." Trust your intuition and let the universal current of life guide you toward understanding the hidden messages of angel numbers. Remember that the interpretation of angel numbers is a deeply personal process, and it is best to do it on your own. After all, it's unique to every person, and who better to understand you than yourself? So, whether you see double, triple, or four-digit sets, the meaning behind the angel number sequences and combinations will never be black and white.

Chapter 4: Other Signs of Angelic Presence

Angels are all around you, protecting, guiding, and teaching you. They are constantly sending messages, but more often than not, people don't notice the signs and think they are just random occurrences. However, nothing is random. Keep your eyes and heart open, and you will spot the messages you are meant to receive.

Angels are always around you. Once you're aware of the signs, this will become clearer to you.
https://creazilla.com/nodes/1712425-guardian-angel-wing-sky-illustration

This chapter covers various angelic signs and symbols and their meanings.

Unexpected Events

You take a day off from work because you must go to the bank. Before you reach your destination, your sister-in-law calls to tell you that your brother has had an accident and that he is in the hospital. You quickly drive there to find that your brother is fine. He only has a couple of bruises and no serious injuries. You are relieved, but it is too late to go to the bank, and you don't know what to do. You look at your phone to find multiple notifications from news apps; there was a shooting at the bank, and nine people were injured. You sit down in shock because you can't believe what happened. This could have been you. You are relieved. Strangely enough, your brother's accident saved your life.

You have probably experienced similar situations where an unexpected event changed your plans, only to find out later it was a blessing. This isn't a mere coincidence; it is the angels' presence in your life protecting you from harm. Sometimes, the angels create unexpected events to push you towards something that will benefit you or away from danger. Remember, angels can't directly interfere with your life since humans have free will. They will only send you symbols, hoping you will decode them and make the right choice.

Coincidences

A coincidence is a series of surprising and meaningful events that don't seem to be connected but are actually related. What seem like insignificant or random events can have a bigger and deeper meaning behind them.

For instance, you got laid off from your job. Even though you never liked it and you always wanted to do something else, you are still upset because you need the work. One day, you are doing your grocery shopping and find a new gym has opened near your home. You decide to join it. You go every day except for Saturdays. One week you get a bad cold and are sick all week. You start to feel better on Saturday, so you go to the gym. There you meet an old college friend. While catching up, you tell them you recently lost your job. Your friend exclaims, "What a coincidence! We have been looking for new people to hire. Why don't you come for an interview?" One week later, you have a new job.

Look at all the coincidences in this story. First, you get laid off, then decide to join the gym, but then you have a cold, so you change your schedule. You then meet an old friend who offers you a job. All of these aren't mere accidents but the work of angels to get you closer to your dream job. Look at your life. You will notice that many small and simple events led you to better things. Trust the process. The angels always have your best interest at heart.

Flashes of Light

Angels are made of light, so it makes sense that they send you flashes or sparkles to inform you of their presence. When one is nearby, you can suddenly see strong light in the corner of your eyes or experience visions of sparkles or shimmers. If you can still see these flashes with your eyes closed, an angel is right by your side. Take a deep breath and be present in the moment. Feel their angelic light around you and let it uplift and heal you.

This light often appears in different colors, depending on the angels communicating with you. It can also signify that the angels are watching over you and protecting you.

Each angel has their own light, but white light is often a symbol of your guardian angel either sending you a message or wanting to get your attention.

Angel Colors

- **Archangel Raphael:** Green
- **Archangel Michael:** Blue
- **Archangel Uriel:** Red
- **Archangel Zadkiel:** Purple
- **Archangel Chamuel:** Pink
- **Archangel Jophiel:** Yellow

Each color can also have a meaning behind it.

- Purple and blue - you are burned out and in need of a break to unwind
- Green symbolizes power
- Orange symbolizes optimism

Disclaimer: Flashes in your vision can result from a health condition. See your doctor whenever you experience this sensation. If there is no medical condition, this can be a sign from your guardian angel.

Bodily Sensations

Physical sensations often occur when an angel is near you. It is a sign of their presence and that they want to communicate with you. You will experience a tingling right above your head in an area called "the crown of the head." That area is connected to the angels' halos. You can also feel a gentle touch on your hand or a slight stroke on your hair, especially when you are sad, depressed, scared, or going through a tough time. The angels will come to comfort you and let you know that you aren't alone and that they will always be here for you. You will also experience these sensations while praying or meditating because, at those moments, your mind is clear, and you can see and feel things on a spiritual level.

As they surround you with their love and positive energy, an angel's presence will bring chills, goosebumps, or a warm feeling. They send you these signals to bring your attention to something, to confirm your thoughts and feelings, or as a sign that you are on your way to something great. For instance, if you experience goosebumps on a date, it can be a sign that this is the right person for you. If you experience chills during a job interview, it means that you will have a future in this place.

Scents

Have you ever experienced a sweet scent or a pleasant fragrance like fruits, flowers, perfume, or your favorite food? The smell will come out of nowhere without any reasonable explanation. This is an angel reaching out to communicate with you. If you notice that the scent is familiar, like the perfume of your late grandfather, it means that the angel is present with his spirit. The angels often approach you with scents that bring warm and loving memories to give you a positive experience.

Coins

Coins are symbols that the universe is going to reward you for your good deeds.
https://unsplash.com/photos/close-up-photo-of-assorted-coins-NeTPASr-bmQ?utm_content=creditShareLink&utm_medium=referral&utm_source=unsplash Photo by Josh Appel on Unsplash

Angels send you coins to let you know that your finances are about to improve and that the universe will reward you for all your good deeds. You can find coins in an old jacket, the street, your home, or any other unexpected place. If you find eleven cents, consider yourself lucky since it is the most significant angel number. This can mean that something great is about to happen. A coin can also carry other messages, so observe all of its details, like the year and material, and you can find the answers you have been seeking. Whenever you find a coin, be happy, and thank the angels as your life is about to change for the better.

Feathers

White feathers are associated with angels, and they often use them to let you know they are nearby or to get your attention. Whenever you feel lost or alone, your guardian angel will send you a message of love and hope so you know everything will eventually be OK. The angels are aware of your struggles and are listening to your prayers. They understand that you need reassurance and want you to know that they are by your side and will always protect you. If you are struggling and about to give up on something, the feather can be a sign to keep going because things are about to get better.

You will usually find these feathers in random and unexpected places like your home, bag, car, or office.

Messages through People

Sometimes, angels will send you messages through other people who aren't even aware of it. These people can either be your friends, family, or complete strangers, like a waiter at a restaurant. They can tell you something you want to hear, especially when you are struggling with a decision or problem and looking for guidance.

Say you are walking down the street with many thoughts rushing through your head. Suddenly, an elderly lady walks by you and smiles, saying, "You will get through this." You might think that this is a random incident or that this woman is crazy, but it's actually a reassuring message your guardian angel sent to ease your concerns.

The angels can also send you warnings to keep you away from a dangerous path. For instance, you plan to get your cat neutered, and you have already found a vet and reserved an appointment. Your sister visits you a day before the operation and tells you that her neighbor's cat passed away while being spayed because the vet made a mistake. She tells you his name, and you realize it is the same vet who is going to neuter your cat. You quickly cancel the appointment and look for another clinic. The angels send you your sister on that day to warn you against the vet to protect your pet.

Voices

Hearing a loud disembodied voice means that misfortune is coming your way, so you must be careful. For example, you are about to cross the street when you hear a loud voice telling you to stop. You take a step back, and a car quickly drives by. Had you not heard the warning, the car would have hit you.

However, not all these messages are negative. Some can be positive. Many healthcare workers who spend time with patients at the end of their lives have said they heard the words "thank you" multiple times just before their patients die. This can be an angel thanking them for their sacrifice and for helping these people at a critical stage in their lives.

Disclaimer: Hearing voices can also result from a mental health condition. See your doctor whenever you experience this sensation. If there is no medical or mental health condition, this can be a sign from your guardian angel.

Dreams

Angels prefer to appear to people in their dreams since it is the easiest way to reach them, and they can send them all kinds of signs and symbols. When you are awake and see a sign or hear a voice, you may question its validity. However, in the dream world, anything is possible, and people are more receptive to messages. Your guardian angel can warn you of a terrible event in the future, like a plane crash, car accident, or getting sick. You can also receive disturbing premonitions about the future. Knowing that something terrible is about to happen or that you or a loved one can be in danger is disconcerting and can cause you a lot of anxiety. However, the angels don't want you to be troubled. They want you to take all the necessary precautions to protect yourself.

Many survivors of terrible events like plane crashes have stated that they had nightmares before the incident. Pay attention to your dreams and if you have real ones that make you feel awful after you wake up, consider it a warning from the angels, and think carefully before making any decision or taking action.

Uncomfortable Feeling in the Solar Plexus

The solar plexus is the third of the seven chakras and is located in the naval area. The angels use this area of the body to send you warning signs since it is very sensitive, and you can easily feel any change or tingling in it. You can feel discomfort, tightening, nausea, or butterflies. You often experience This gut feeling when something doesn't feel right. Always pay attention to your body and never ignore these sensations. Once you experience something, be vigilant.

Say you have a job interview, and the moment you arrive at the company, you feel a tightening in your stomach. That can signal that this isn't the right place for you. You can also feel queasy or creeped out by certain people. That means they aren't good individuals and don't have your best interest at heart, so you should be careful whenever you are around them.

Don't be scared of these warnings; they are meant to provide guidance and alert you to negative people, places, and events.

Disclaimer: Discomfort or tightening in your chest area or feeling nauseous could be the result of a health condition. See your doctor whenever you experience this sensation. If there is no medical condition, this can be a sign from your guardian angel.

Car Trouble or Delays

Angels often use unexplainable car troubles to get your attention, teach you a lesson, or keep you away from harm. They only want to slow you down for a few minutes or hours until the danger passes. For example, you are on your way to the airport, but your car breaks down, delaying you for twenty minutes. When you arrive, you find that you missed your flight. You are angry and frustrated. However, you discover later that the plane crashed and there are no survivors. Your guardian angel only delayed you to save your life. Don't get angry whenever you miss any opportunity. There is always a hidden meaning or a blessing behind it.

Songs

Angels use recurring songs to reach out to you and send you specific messages. For instance, the radio plays the same song daily on your way to work. Even when you shuffle music on Spotify, you constantly keep getting that one song. If this has ever happened to you, listen carefully to the lyrics and notice the theme, as they can have a meaning behind them. The songs can be reassuring, reaffirm your feelings, or make you feel better, especially if you are going through something. You are in an Uber and considering whether to break up with your boyfriend when the song "Get Another Boyfriend" by the Backstreet Boys plays, and this lyric gets your attention "Now this must come to an end, get another boyfriend." Some lyrics can be straightforward, while others provide a clue relating to your experience.

Temperature

If you feel a change in your body's temperature, you are probably surrounded by angels. You might experience pressure in the back of your neck, feel a tingle on your head, get chills, or feel cold. You might also feel like you are surrounded by a warm light. These sensations shouldn't distress or frighten you and can often feel like a normal experience. You will feel safe because you are in the presence of angels.

Rainbow

Whenever people witness a rainbow, they always feel they are in the presence of something magical. This beautiful natural phenomenon is associated with angels. Your guardian angel can send you a message of love, support, and hope whenever you feel disconnected from the universe or if nothing is going your way. They want to open your eyes to the beauty of nature and remind you that there is so much in life to live for and enjoy. The rainbow is always a symbol of beauty and positivity.

Ringing in Your Right Ear

Angels often communicate with you by making your right ear ring. That is because it is connected to the spirit world. Receiving a message in this ear will surely catch your attention. If the ringing is long and high-pitched, the angels want you to know they are with you and will guide you in all your future endeavors. A short, loud, and sudden ringing is usually a warning. Your guardian angel is worried about you and wants you to reevaluate your life. Perhaps you are about to make a bad decision, and the angels want you to slow down and take your time.

Disclaimer: A ringing in your right ear can result from a health condition. See your doctor whenever you experience this sensation. If there is no medical condition, this can be a sign from your guardian angel.

Clouds

Look up to the sky. There can be a message for you in the clouds. Spend some time in nature, sit silently, and watch the clouds. You can see shapes or symbols like flowers, hearts, or numbers. Those are positive messages sent to encourage and support you. You might find a shape that catches your attention or relates to your current struggles or experience. Say you are considering whether to propose to your girlfriend or not, and you see a heart in the cloud. That indicates that proposing is the right decision.

Direct Messages

Some of the signs can be clear and straightforward and appear in the form of text. Books, billboard signs, ads, or blogs can provide answers to questions you have been pondering. For instance, a book falls from your shelf and opens on a specific page. When you read it, you find that it's a passage that relates to something significant in your life. If you keep seeing the same text in various places, this can be a message worth pondering.

Phone Calls

You are sitting watching TV, and an old high school friend comes to mind. Suddenly, your phone rings, and it is that friend. This isn't a coincidence or a random incident. Your guardian angel has prompted this person to call you because they can give you advice on a current issue, or you just need this person in your life right now.

Pets and Babies

Animals and babies are able to see into the spiritual world. Have you ever seen your pet following around something invisible or your baby smiling for no reason? They are probably looking at an angel.

Animals

Many animals, like dragonflies, butterflies, robins, and hummingbirds, are connected to angels. If you randomly encounter any of them, it can be a message from your guardian angel. Seeing a robin in an unexpected place can mean that the spirit of a loved one is resting in peace and is in a better place.

Strong Intuition

Whenever you are in the presence of an angel, you will feel more alive. Everything around you will look more beautiful and colorful, and your intuition will be heightened. Your gut feeling will always be right, and you will have the ability to feel other people's emotions and empathize with them.

You Aren't Alone

Have you ever felt that you aren't alone and that someone is in the room with you? Perhaps you feel that someone is sitting next to you on the couch or lying beside you in bed. However, this doesn't bother or scare you. An angel's presence will make you feel loved, safe, and warm. You will often experience this sensation when you feel misunderstood, isolated, or stressed. Your guardian angel wants you to know that you are never alone and they are always walking beside you.

You are loved, supported, guided, and never alone. These are the most common messages angels want to convey. Your guardian angel will never give up on you. They will keep sending you symbols and signs to provide assistance in every aspect of your life.

Each symbol they send has a meaning behind it, but only you can decode it. Think of them in the context of your personal experiences, and you will surely find the answers you seek.

Chapter 5: Angelic Symbols and Sigils

Since this book heavily embraces symbolism, the topic of angelic symbols is inevitable. This chapter introduces the symbols and sigils of a variety of angels (putting high emphasis on the Archangels). It also provides several exercises like meditations, prayers, and other forms of spiritual practices that can be used with angelic symbols and sigils.

What Are Angelic Symbols, Signs, and Sigils?

Many people view angelic signs and symbols as a way to identify if and how an angel is communicating with them. However, they can also be quite useful if you want to call on an angel and connect with them. As spiritual beings, angels act as messengers between people and entities on a higher spiritual level. Therefore, they require specific means of communication, a unique language of symbols. Whether you seek their assistance to resolve an issue in your life, comfort, or guidance for moving forward with your life, angelic symbols, and sigils can help you get your message across. Working with angelic symbolism in conjunction with mindfulness exercises and techniques that empower spiritual growth is recommended. Suppose you notice a specific symbol or sign appearing around you. In that case, you can decipher its meaning through meditation, similar mindfulness, and growth-inducing exercises.

Angelic sigils and symbols depict the entity or force associated with them. They are simple patterns made to represent specific intentions or names. The sigil of an Archangel is also viewed as their signature, as these beings specialize in specific forms of assistance they can provide. Not only are the sigils for Archangels derived from letters of names of entities they represent, but they also often look like a monogram.

Symbols Associated with Angels

Here is a list of some well-known angels and their symbols.

Archangel Michael

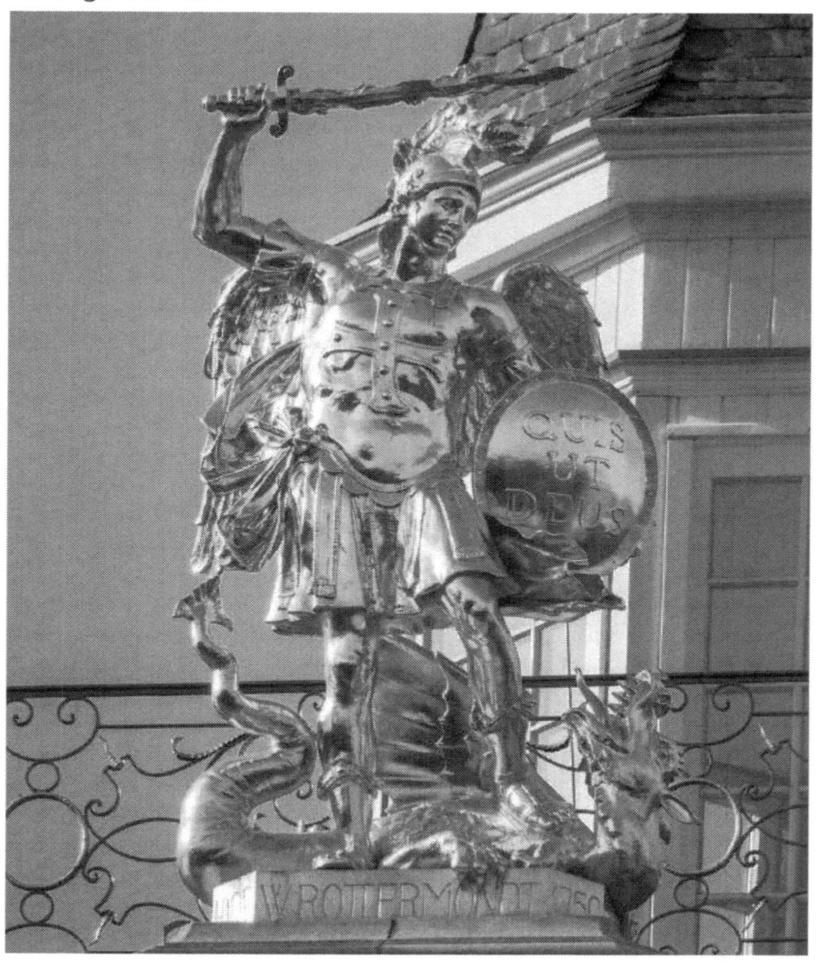

Archangel Michael is a warrior; many symbols indicate protection and guidance.

https://www.wallpaperflare.com/angel-soldier-archangel-michael-archangel-michael-combative-wallpaper-etybt

As the leader of all Archangels, Michael is depicted as a Warrior of Light. His symbols include:

- **A sword:** It depicts the cutting of bonds from evil and protection from harm. It also expresses strength and courage.
- **Personal items of empowerment:** The angel can guide you on your path to success with many tools. You can use any tool that represents strength, protection, integrity, courage, or success to you.
- **Money:** Financial empowerment and security.
- **Doorways and crossroads:** As the most powerful angel, Michael can shield you and open any door for you.
- **A spear:** This has a similar significance as the sword. It gives you spiritual strength, courage, and protection. It also helps you overcome difficulties or find a new direction in life.
- **Red tape:** This is often depicted on top of the sword or spear but can also appear alone. It spiritually empowers you or your tools.

Archangel Uriel

Often said to be the wisest of all Archangels, Uriel is known for his bright intellect. He can also serve as a source of inspiration, help resolve urgent issues, and empower your magical skills.

Uriel can be symbolized by:

- **Light:** The angel is known as the Prince of Light, and his brightness can illuminate your path toward a happy and fulfilling life. Candlelight is the most well-known symbol of Uriel.
- **A scale:** This item denotes that Uriel can help you resolve dilemmas and find the appropriate answers for difficult moral or spiritual questions.
- **Personal items of joy:** With the right tool, Uriel can help you find joy in life. You can use anything that brings you happiness.
- **Tools for divination:** Being a wise angel, Uriel can provide you with transformative ideas during divination. These can be any tools that help you gain information about the past, present, or future.

- **Tools for spiritual enlightenment:** Items you use for spiritual empowerment can also represent Uriel.
- **A sword:** Sometimes, Uriel is depicted with a sword. It indicates he can help you make urgent decisions and resolve your problems.

Archangel Raphael

The kindest of all angels, Archangel Raphael is an incredibly gentle being who can heal your mind, body, and soul. Also known as the Angel of Providence, he can help you chase away anxiety and depression and overcome despair even during the most trying of times.

Raphael is symbolized by:

- **Items representing self-love:** You can use these items to remind you of your strengths and values.
- **Alabaster jar:** Indicating Raphael's ability to provide healing or relief from traumas affecting you or your loved ones. You can use any type of jar that can hold medicine.
- **Wounded or healed animals:** Raphael is also believed to be kind to animals, and using animals that need healing or have recently healed can be a great way to connect with this angel.
- **Items representing personal safety:** Raphael can help you stay safe during your travels and risky ventures.
- **Donations:** Giving back to the community can also be an excellent way to build a connection to this Archangel.

Archangel Gabriel

The Archangel Gabriel is linked to communication, purity, and the protection of your space. He can help you cleanse your thoughts, emotions, and resulting actions.

Gabriel is symbolized by:

- **A trumpet:** Depicting the divine voice and the messages that carry good news and promise change for the better.
- **Books and literature:** Gabriel is the guardian of your thoughts, words, and behavior. Using the right piece of literature to express your feelings, you can summon him to your aid when you feel hurt, agitated, or confused.

- **Mail, news, and other symbols of communication:** Using these, you can get Gabriel to provide you with some good news in tough times.
- **The four elements:** Linked to transformation and the purity of nature. These are traditionally used for home protection.
- **Mirrors:** They illustrate divine wisdom and a hidden mystery. They are great for self-reflection and discovering your inner power.
- **A lantern:** It empowers spiritual works and helps protect you, your space, and your loved ones. A lantern with a light flickering inside can also depict the heart, the core of a family home that keeps the family together.

Archangel Metatron

Known for his quick thinking ability, the Archangel Metatron is usually symbolized by lightning. This depicts how the angel can guide you when making fast and critical decisions. It can help you get to the core of the matter fast and without risking making a misstep. With this symbol, you will always have the security of Metratron guiding you in the right direction.

Archangel Raziel

As the Archangel associated with magic, Raziel is a source of inspiration for any type of magical or spiritual work. You can use cauldrons, spellbooks, wands, and other tools of magic and symbols to summon Raziel when you feel stuck or don't know how to overcome a challenge in magical or spiritual work. Items or people you find inspiring for your pursuits can also be used to connect with Raziel.

Archangel Sandalphon

This is the Archangel that offers clarity when you're at a crossroads. He can also provide protection from evil spiritual influences. Salphadon is symbolized by:

- **White candles**: They counteract dark energies.
- **Salt:** It can purify your mind, body, soul, and tools from negative energies.
- **Purifying herbs**: They cleanse you and your space from confusing or negative thoughts and influences.

Archangel Jegudiel

Known as the divine Glorifier, Jegudiel is the Archangel of clarity. He is symbolized by:

A golden wreath: Holding this symbol in your right hand, you can summon this angel to gain clarity and see things in a better light.

Working with Angelic Symbols and Sigils

When you work with angels, remember that you might require a different form of assistance at specific times of your life. Archangels have distinctive areas in which they can offer aid, whereas lesser angels might help you in various matters. Your guardian angel might guide you toward a better path, or if they can't help you, they will offer direction to an Archangel.

While your guardian angel can be called on for anything you need - at any time - it is best to invoke an Archangel only when you've got an urgent need and are prepared to make powerful changes in your life. Be clear with your intent when deciding which symbols or sigils to use. The more specific your intention is, the more suitable your choice of symbols will be, and the better an angel will be able to respond in turn.

Whether you use the symbols alongside prayers, meditation, or another spiritually empowering exercise, choose the one that feels right and works for you based on your values.

Arm yourself with patience when using angelic symbols and sigils. For beginners, they rarely will work instantly. In most cases, you'll need lots of practice and repetition. The changes will begin to appear more slowly. Depending on what is best for you at any moment of your life, you might need to wait a significant amount of time until you see the results of your work. However, trust the angels to bring the best possible outcome for you, even if you initially find it confusing.

Angelic Sigils

A sigil is a symbol corresponding to specific angels, although they're typically used to call on higher beings like Archangels. While there are premade sigils, these are designed based on their general meaning and significance to the author. Of course, you can use them to better understand angelic sigils, but making your own will create a more personal connection to the angels. Whether you opt for copying ready-made sigils or creating your own, your first step is to learn how to draw a sigil. Once you master this, you can charge the sigil with the energy of the associated Archangel.

Here is how to create angelic sigils:

1. Take a premade template or create your own. Either way, you'll use the letters of the name of the Archangel you'd like to invoke or the intention that corresponds with the angel.
2. For example, to call on Archangel Michael first, write down the letter M, the first letter of his name. Then repeat until you reach the last letter. Similarly, if you want protection, you start by writing down the letter P.
3. After writing all letters in the intention or name, connect them by drawing lines between them. It's up to you in which format you write the letters or the connecting lines.
4. Once you've connected all of the letters, your sigil is finished.

It's crucial to remember that working with angelic symbols and sigils is highly personal and subjective. A sign that holds significance for one person can be entirely meaningless to another. Trust your intuition and inner guide when interpreting and using angelic symbols and sigils. Also, remember that angels often use distinct symbols to communicate with you at different times, depending on your unique needs and circumstances. It's critical to remain open-minded when working with angelic symbolism. Even the same sign and sigil can have different meanings depending on the circumstances. Sometimes, the significance of a symbol will be more direct. Other times, it will be subtle and open to interpretation. Angelic symbols and sigils can be excellent tools for gaining insight and guidance from angels. The knowledge you gain will aid your spiritual growth and help you navigate your life with ease. By combining these signs with spiritual exercises, you'll learn to trust the angels and yourself more, which will help you overcome any challenge and achieve any goal in life.

How to Use Your Angel Sigil

In most cases, you will need a ritual to prepare your mind to focus on the specific sigil. This involves letting your intent known and calling out an angel's name three times to open the line of communication. Lace your intention with hope and have an open heart, as this helps form an unbreakable link between you and the angel. It creates an organic bond that enables you to work with them freely.

Bringing Angelic Energy into Your Life

As you've seen above, to bring the energy of an Archangel into your life, you must create a sigil by arranging the letters of their name or specialty into an easily visualized symbol. The second step is to imprint the sigil into your subconscious.

Here is how to do it:

1. Gaze into the sigil and repeat its name.
2. Focus on your breathing and keep repeating the sigil's name until it becomes a mantra.

Next, you'll need to connect it to the angel:

1. Draw the sigil on a piece of paper and place it on your altar, surrounding it with crystals, the representation of the angel, and their correspondences.
2. Focusing on the sigil and the angel's name, summon them.

Once you've established the connection between the angel and the sigil, you'll need to repress your conscious memory of the symbol. Make a deliberate effort to forget about it, as sigil work can be influenced by the desires and thoughts of the conscious mind.

Ritual for Better Focus

You can summon an angel by focusing on the sigil and envisioning it being connected to the angel's essence during meditation. You can use their power to empower yourself with better focus during the exercise and gain mental clarity to manifest your intent.

Instructions:

1. On a piece of paper, draw the sigil.
2. Next, light the candles and place them in front of you. Turn off all artificial lights.
3. Place the sigil between the candles.
4. Then, reflect on the meaning it has for you at that moment.
5. Visualize the sigil growing bigger and more brilliant, eventually glowing brighter than the candles around it.
6. Keep the image in front of you until you're comfortable or you gain the mental clarity you need.

Prayers to Archangels

When calling on an Archangel with a prayer, their symbol or sigil can serve as an excellent channeling tool. All you need is a clear intention and an open mind to interpret the messages you'll receive after contacting them.

Instructions:

1. Start by setting clear intentions. Define what you want to obtain by invoking an Archangel; remember, they all have their specialties. For example, call on Archangel Michael if you require spiritual protection and empowerment.
2. The next step is ensuring that you're properly calling on them. If you haven't worked with the angel before, tap into your intuition and see whether you have the correct tools.
3. Once you've defined your intention and know that you're using adequate tools, you can address the angel with the following prayer:

"Dear (the Archangel you wish to invoke).

I stand here as your humble follower.

I ask you to (the angel's specialty).

Please come to me and send your divine blessings to those I care about."

Meditation Tools

There are several ways you can use angelic symbols and sigils for meditation. Here are some suggestions on what to do when meditating with angelic symbols:

- Express gratitude for the angel's presence in your life and the messages they send you.
- Thank the angel for their guidance and support. Reiterate your trust in their ability to shield and direct you through challenging times.
- Ask for guidance and support if you need it at that specific time.
- Express your desire to deepen your connection with an angel.
- Tap into your intuition to hone in. This will help you trust it more when deciding which symbols and sigils to use or interpreting the ones the angels send you.

- If you are unsure of which action to take after communicating with an angel, use mediation to contact them again to clarify whether they want to make a change, be more present, or take another action.

Instructions:

1. Sit comfortably and take the angelic sigil or symbol into your hands.
2. Focus on taking deep breaths and empty your mind of all thoughts.
3. Visualize an angel (or symbol or sign) in your mind's eye. Imagine them as powerful beings of light.
4. Then, ask them to encircle you with their essence and protection.
5. Remain in this state for as long as you feel comfortable.
6. When you're finished, thank the angel for his presence.

Using Angelic Symbols and Sigils as Charms

Another way to use angelic symbols and sigils is to carry them as talismans or charms. You can wear them as a bracelet, necklace, or earrings or keep them in your pocket. These are all great ways to keep a symbol (and its power) close to your personal space. While most charms and talismans are used for luck and protection, you can also hold them during meditation and other mindfulness exercises. You can empower the symbols and sigils with intent, and looking at the object will remind you of your intention anytime you need it. Charms and talismans can also be displayed in your space. This works great if you need an angel's power to protect your home or workspace or require guidance in matters that concern these spaces. Whether you display them on your altar and use them as a channeling tool to invoke angels or on a table or shelf where you spend a lot of time, they'll remind you of the angel's presence and power.

Clarification Meditation and Prayer

If you are unsure what a specific symbol you've encountered means or which sigils you should use to contact an angel, you can ask the angels themselves. Keep the signs you discover or learn from angels in a journal to track your experiences. Once you understand the meaning of the signs, note them as well in the journal.

Instructions:

1. Sit comfortably and take the chosen sigil or symbol into your hands.
2. Focusing on bringing an angel close to you, address them with the following prayer:

   "Dear angel, I invite you into my hearth and home.

   Please surround me with your love, light, and protection.

   Help me interpret the symbols I encounter and use.

   Guide my intuition to uncover the meaning I need.

   Help me understand them with clarity and wisdom.

   Please bless me with the strength and courage I need

   To follow the instructions, I can gain through the symbols and sigils.

   Help me trust the symbols to lead me toward my purpose.

   Thank you for the support and blessings you've bestowed upon me.

   I trust in your guidance."
3. After reciting the prayer, meditate as long as you need to gain clarity on a specific symbol or sigil.
4. Feel the angel's presence fill you with peace, love, and understanding as you meditate. Feel their guidance and protection.
5. Once you've gained clarity on a symbol, use it according to its meaning to you at that specific time in your life.

Chapter 6: Synchronicity, Divine Timing, and Coincidence

Do you always happen to look at the time when it's 11:11? Perhaps you've seen a specific sequence of numbers multiple times throughout your day. These are known as angel numbers and are believed to be messages from the divine realm. Angel numbers are often associated with synchronicity and divine timing, as they tend to appear during significant moments in life. Some may dismiss them as mere coincidences, but those who believe in the power of angel numbers see them as a sign of guidance and support from the universe.

This chapter will explore the concepts of synchronicity, divine timing, and coincidence. It will examine the history and theory of synchronicity, along with instructions on how to manifest it. It will also discuss the concept of divine timing and its connection with free will versus fate, as well as list various signs which indicate divine timing. Lastly, it will define what a coincidence is, set it apart from synchronicity, and list the various categories of synchronicity with examples. Ultimately, this chapter will help you understand these concepts and how to use them for self-exploration and spiritual growth.

Embracing Synchronicity: Aligning Your Actions with the Universe

Do you ever find yourself experiencing coincidences that seem too perfect to be mere chance? Maybe you were thinking about someone, and then they called you out of the blue. Or, you stumbled on a book that addressed a problem you were struggling with after silently wishing for answers. These meaningful and seemingly impossible coincidences are called synchronicities and are believed to be powerful signs from the universe. This section will explore synchronicity's history, theory, manifestation, and how-tos. With this knowledge, you'll be better equipped to align your actions with the universe and transform your life meaningfully.

History and Theory

Swiss psychiatrist Carl Jung first introduced synchronicity in the 1920s. Jung noticed that certain coincidences were too significant to be explained by chance and believed these events had psychological significance. He coined the term *synchronicity* to describe them and emphasized the importance of paying attention to them as they could reveal deeper insights about the unconscious mind.

Carl Jung introduced the concept of synchronicity.
https://picryl.com/media/eth-bib-jung-carl-gustav-1875-1961-portrait-portr-14163-cropped-c7875d

The theory of synchronicity depends on the concept of the collective unconscious, which is a reservoir of experiences and psychic knowledge shared by all humans. According to Jung, synchronicity occurs when two events, one from the individual's unconscious and another from the collective unconscious, align meaningfully. For instance, an individual struggling to make a decision may encounter a stranger who unknowingly can provide insight into the matter.

Today, synchronicity remains relevant in modern spiritual practices. Meditation, for example, can help individuals increase self-awareness and tap into their unconscious minds for insights. Tarot card reading and astrology are other practices that use the principles of synchronicity to provide guidance and enlightenment. These practices allow individuals to embrace the randomness of life and welcome synchronicities as a means of growth and development.

The power of synchronicity in spiritual practices is not limited to self-discovery alone. Consistently experiencing synchronicities can indicate that an individual is on the right path and can provide reassurance that their goals and objectives are aligned with their purpose. Being open to synchronistic events, even if they seem insignificant, can lead to profound shifts in perspective and greater faith in the universe's ability to guide and support.

Manifestation of Synchronicity

Synchronicity manifests in several ways, including coincidences, telepathy, dreams, and symbols. For example, synchronicity could be experienced when you keep seeing the same sequence of numbers over and over again. Other times, it could appear in your relationships by meeting someone with the same name or birthday. It can even manifest through life-changing events like job opportunities, discovering a newfound passion, or a chance encounter.

Synchronicity can sometimes be as simple as seeing the same number repeatedly or meeting someone with the same name as you. Other times, it can lead to significant discoveries and breakthroughs in your personal and professional life.

Aligning with Synchronicity

Aligning with synchronicity is about cultivating an open mind and heart regarding the universe's signs. When you are open to possibilities and opportunities, the universe sends you synchronistic events that align with your path. You can practice aligning with synchronicity by trusting your intuition, listening to your gut, and paying attention to signs and symbols. Cultivating a daily practice such as meditation or journaling can help you become more self-aware and tuned into the universe's messages.

How to Harness the Power of Synchronicity

To truly take advantage of the power of synchronicity, you must learn to co-create with the universe. This means taking inspired action toward your goals but also allowing the universe to guide you through synchronistic events. You can practice co-creating by setting intentions, clearly defining your goals, and taking action. With this approach, opportunities and synchronicities will begin to appear in your life in no time.

When tuned into the world around you, you'll be more likely to recognize patterns and make connections you may have missed before. You can also try practicing meditation or visualization techniques to help you focus your mind and connect with your intuition. Another essential aspect of synchronicity is being aware of your thoughts and emotions. If you're fixated on negative feelings and beliefs, you'll be more likely to attract negative experiences. On the other hand, if you focus on positivity and abundance, you'll be more open to synchronistic events that bring you happiness and fulfillment.

Benefits of Embracing Synchronicity

Embracing synchronicity has the potential to enhance all aspects of your life. When you begin to pay attention to the subtle cues and follow the signs from the universe, you'll notice that opportunities for personal and professional growth arise more frequently. As a result, life becomes more abundant, and you'll experience fewer struggles. You'll also notice that synchronicity brings people who are aligned with your values and vision into your life, making your relationships more meaningful.

- **Shift Your Perspective:** Embracing synchronicity can help you shift your perspective on life. It can help you see the hidden meaning behind events and circumstances. This shift allows you to stay positive in difficult situations and see the opportunities that come your way. By embracing synchronicity, you learn to see life as a journey filled with wonder, curiosity, and discoveries. You learn to trust that the universe is conspiring to bring you to your highest good.

- **Experience More Positivity and Optimism:** Embracing synchronicity can also bring more positivity and optimism into your life. By seeing the connections between events, you begin to believe that everything happens for a reason. This belief can lead to a more positive attitude toward life. You begin to see challenges as opportunities for growth and learning. You learn to trust that everything will work out in the end. This positivity and optimism can help you attract more positive experiences and people into your life.
- **Lead a Happier and More Fulfilling Life:** By seeing the connections between events and circumstances in your life, you begin to see the bigger picture of your life story. You begin to understand that everything that has happened to you, good or bad, has led you to where you are today. By trusting synchronicity, you can let go of worry and doubt and embrace life's adventures, leading to a greater sense of peace, purpose, and happiness.
- **Connect With Others:** By seeing the connections between events in your life, you begin to see the connections between you and others. You begin to realize that we are all in this together, experiencing similar challenges and triumphs. This can lead to a greater sense of empathy and compassion. By seeing the connections between ourselves and others, we can build more meaningful relationships and create a more compassionate world.
- **Helps you Trust the Universe:** Finally, embracing synchronicity can help you trust the universe. By seeing the connections between events in your life, you begin to trust that everything is happening for a reason. You begin to trust that the universe is working to bring you to your highest good. By trusting the universe, you can let go of worry and doubt and embrace the adventure of life.

The Power of Divine Timing: Understanding Universal Rules and Free Will

Have you ever had a moment when everything seemed to line up perfectly? A moment when you achieved exactly what you always wanted, or an unexpected opportunity appeared that changed your life completely? That is the power of divine timing. It's the universe's way of orchestrating events to perfectly align with your highest good. This section will explore divine timing, the universal rules governing it, and the age-old debate of free will versus fate.

Definition

Divine timing refers to the idea that the universe has a plan for your life and that everything happens when the time is right. It's the belief that nothing in your life happens by chance and that each moment unfolds precisely as it's meant to. Whether meeting the right person at the right time, getting a job offer that changes everything, or simply feeling a sense of flow, it's all part of the universe's plan for you.

Universal Rules of Divine Timing

We've all heard the saying "timing is everything," but have you ever stopped to think about how true that statement is? Many of us have experienced situations where things just seemed to fall into place at the exact right moment or where no matter how much we try to make something happen, it just doesn't seem to be the right time. This is because there are universal rules to divine timing that we all must follow, whether we are aware of them or not. These are the universal rules of divine timing and how you can use them to your advantage in your personal and professional life.

1. **Everything Happens in Its Own Time:** The first rule of divine timing is that everything happens when it is meant to happen. This means that you cannot force or rush anything in your life. If you try to make something happen before it is time, you will only create resistance and push it further away. Instead, trust that the universe has its timeline and that everything will come to fruition when it is supposed to.
2. **Everything Happens for a Reason:** Even the most difficult, painful moments have a purpose that may not be immediately clear. The universe has a way of using these moments to teach us valuable lessons and to help us grow and evolve. Understanding that everything happens for a reason can bring peace and acceptance to difficult times. The key is to try to stay open-minded and trust that the universe always has your best interests.

3. **Everything Is Interconnected:** The universe constantly works to create harmony and balance, so things often fall into place when we least expect it. This is because everything in the universe is interconnected, and when one thing is out of balance, it often leads to something else falling into place. Pay attention to the subtle cues and synchronicities that appear in your life. They could be guiding you toward something bigger. Following the clues can lead you to unexpected opportunities that could completely transform your life.
4. **The Universe Supports Your Desires:** The universe constantly works to bring you closer to your desires, but sometimes that takes time. When you focus on what you want and take action, the universe will support you every step of the way. It's just a matter of trusting in the process and being patient. You will eventually be rewarded with what you seek when you align with your desires.
5. **The Law of Attraction:** This universal law states that what we focus on and think about will eventually come into our lives. This means that if you are constantly worrying and thinking negative thoughts, you will create more of the same in your life. However, staying focused on what you want and keeping your thoughts positive will create the opportunities needed to manifest your desires.

It can be easy to get caught up in comparing our lives to others and feeling like we are not where we are supposed to be. But the truth is that we are all on our unique paths and timeline. Trust that the timing of your life is perfect and that everything is happening as it should. Remember that setbacks and challenges are only temporary and are necessary for growth and learning.

Understanding the Age-Old Debate of Free Will Versus Fate

This debate has been raging for centuries. Philosophers, religious leaders, scientists, and even writers have discussed this age-old argument between determinism and the notion of individual control. But what exactly is free will, and how does it differ from fate?

Free will is the ability to make choices that are not predetermined. It's the notion that we can make decisions that are not influenced by anything but our desires, values, and beliefs. It is often associated with the idea of personal responsibility and the ability to choose our destiny. On the other hand, fate is the belief that our life is predetermined and that there is nothing we can do to change our destiny. This means that no matter how much we try, our life will always follow a set path already laid out for us.

Despite their apparent differences, many philosophers suggest that free will and fate might not be mutually exclusive. For example, the concept of determinism suggests that past experiences and genetic makeup influence our actions and decisions. However, determinists do not necessarily believe that our lives are predetermined. Instead, they suggest that our choices are limited by factors we cannot control, such as environmental factors, social norms, and cultural values.

Another concept that supports the idea of free will and fate coexisting is the notion of compatibilism. Proponents of compatibilism argue that free will and determinism are not mutually exclusive but work together to shape our decisions and actions. They suggest that, even if external factors influence our choices, we can still act freely if we believe that we are making our own decisions based on our desires and beliefs.

Despite the arguments presented by determinists and compatibilists, many people still hold on to the belief in personal control and free will. They believe that they are the sole drivers of their life and that their actions significantly impact the outcome of their lives. These individuals are more likely to take responsibility for their decisions and are less likely to be influenced by external factors.

The debate between free will and fate is complex and cannot be easily or neatly resolved. While some believe life is predetermined, others argue that people can shape their destiny through their choices. While we may never know the answer to this age-old question, what is essential is that we continue to make our own decisions and strive to take control of our lives. After all, in the end, our choices shape who we are and ultimately determine the course of our lives.

Coincidences

Have you ever experienced a moment when something you were thinking about suddenly happened? Or a time when you ran into someone you were just thinking about? These moments are what we call *coincidences*, and they happen to us quite often. At times, these coincidences can be so eerie that they leave us in amazement, wondering if there's a higher force at work. Let's explore the world of coincidences and synchronicities and what they mean.

Definition

Coincidence is a remarkable occurrence of two or more events or circumstances happening simultaneously without any apparent causal connection. Simply put, it's when two things happen simultaneously by chance. Coincidences are often seen as random occurrences, but some people believe in the idea of synchronicities or meaningful coincidences.

The Difference between Coincidences and Synchronicities

Unlike coincidences, Carl Jung believed synchronicities had a deeper meaning or purpose. Synchronistic events are experiences where there is no direct causal relationship between two or more seemingly related events, but they occur together in a way that is meaningful to the person experiencing them. In simpler terms, while coincidences are random occurrences, synchronicity is the universe's way of sending us signs and messages.

Categories of Synchronicities

While synchronicities may seem random, they often fall into distinct categories that can shed light on their deeper meaning. This section will explore three categories of synchronicities, including acausal parallelism, simultaneity, and unfolding.

1. **Acausal Parallelism:** This category of synchronicity involves a meaningful coincidence between two events that have no causal relationship. For example, you may be walking down the street and cross paths with a stranger who happens to be wearing the same shirt as you. While this may seem like a coincidence, it becomes more meaningful if you later discover that you and the stranger share a common interest or hobby. This type of synchronicity suggests that there is a deeper order or intelligence at work in the universe, guiding us towards connections and experiences that are meant to be.
2. **Simultaneity:** This type of synchronicity involves two or more events occurring simultaneously but not causally related. For example, you may be reading a book and come across a passage that mentions a specific song, only to hear that same song playing on the radio moments later. This type of synchronicity often feels like a sign or message from the universe, offering guidance or confirmation of your decision.

It can also remind us that everything is connected and that we are part of a larger cosmic dance.

3. **Unfolding:** This category of synchronicity involves a sequence of events that unfolds over time, leading to a meaningful outcome. For example, you may have a series of unrelated dreams or encounters that later merge into a new opportunity or direction in your life. This type of synchronicity can be challenging to recognize at the moment, as it often requires patience and trust that things are unfolding as they should. However, it can be a powerful reminder to stay open to new experiences and follow the path that feels right, even if it doesn't make sense at the time.
4. **Tone of Voice:** Lastly, synchronicities can also be categorized by the tone or feeling they evoke. For example, they can be upbeat and joyful, signaling a positive shift or alignment in your life. Conversely, they can be sobering or bittersweet, indicating a challenge or lesson that needs to be learned. Being attuned to the tone of synchronicities can help you understand their meaning and interpret the message they hold for you.

Synchronicities are a fascinating and mysterious aspect of human experience, offering a glimpse into the deeper workings of the universe. By exploring the categories of acausal parallelism, simultaneity, unfolding, and tone, we can begin to make sense of these experiences and tap into their wisdom and guidance. Whether you view synchronicities as divine messages or simply random coincidences, they can be a powerful reminder of the interconnectedness and beauty of all things.

Coincidences and synchronicities are fascinating subjects that can't be fully explained. While some people believe these phenomena are random, others see them as meaningful events sent by the universe or a higher power. Whether coincidences or synchronicities, they remind us that we're all connected and that there may be forces beyond our understanding at work behind the scenes. Whatever the case may be, these experiences can bring us moments of joy, inspiration, and awe, and that alone makes them worth noticing. So, next time you encounter a coincidence or synchronicity, take a moment to appreciate the divine timing and see if it might hold a deeper meaning for you.

Chapter 7: Angelic Correspondences

So far, you've learned that angels are associated with numbers, sequences, symbols, and sigils. However, these aren't the only angelic correspondences that exist. Angels can also be linked to other items and concepts, like days of the week, hours of the day, zodiac signs, colors, months, gemstones, and more. This chapter goes over all these correspondences for several angels.

Michael

As the ruler of the Sun, Archangel Michael is associated with Sunday. Due to the Sun's influence, Michael can illuminate your path and inspire you in many aspects of your life. His abilities are also linked to your individual creative spirit. He is a magnificent source of empowerment and a guardian for those aiming to make a difference in the world. If you want to create something unique without compromising your values, Michael can help you with all your creative endeavors.

Flowers, herbs, and trees to use when working with Archangel Michael include angelica, tagetes, blueweed, sunflower, carnation, St John's wort, celandine, saffron, centaury, rowan blossoms, eyebright, peony, goldenseal, orange blossoms, heliotrope, marigold, hibiscus, chamomile, willow, red sandalwood, celandine, bay, cyclamen, calamus root, cowslip, hops, and mistletoe.

In Tarot, Michael is linked to the cards Strength and Judgment. This indicates his vast influence over the development of life. He governs your ambitions and your mental and physical development. Due to the influence of the Judgement card, Michel can greatly help those seeking repentance, fulfillment, or wanting to express righteousness or mercy. He can help you fend off evil influences but will also impart justice on souls when needed.

Other Associations

Hours of the day and night:

- The 1st and 8th hours of the day and the 3rd and 10th hours of the night on Sunday
- The 5th and 12th hours of the day and the 7th hour of the day on Monday.
- The 2nd and 9th hours of the day and the 4th and 11th hours of the night on Tuesday.
- The 6th hour of the day and the 1st and 8th hours of the night on Wednesday.
- The 3rd and 10th hours of the day and the 5th and 12th hours of the night on Thursday.
- The 7th hour of the day and the 2nd and 9th hours of the night on Friday.
- The 4th and 11th hours of the day and the 6th hour of the night on Saturday.

Element and mode: Fire - Fixed.

Season: Summer - Winter.

Month: August.

Metals: Gold.

Color: Yellow, yellowish green, gold, white.

Crystals: Golden topaz, citrine, diamond, clear quartz, opal, and amber.

Animals: Peacock, eagle, lion, griffin, and wolf.

Body part: Spine, heart, arms, and wrist.

Incense: Orange, olibanum, and frankincense.

Harmonious signs: Aries and Sagittarius.

Deities: Demeter, Venus, Vishnu, Selket, and Horus.

Ages ruled: All ages.

Gabriel

The Governor of the Moon, Archangel Gabriel, is associated with Monday. Due to the Moon's influence, this angel can bring increased spiritual awareness and elevate your mystical experiences, whether you're journeying to the spiritual world, astral travel, or doing dreamwork. He can also solidify your intent through prayer and meditation, especially if you're performing these under the moonlight, outside, and close to a body of water. He can help you establish deep spiritual connections in any environment, from work to community to close-knit family. Gabriel can also protect you when traveling across water, against bad weather, or when you feel sorrow. The Moon helps remove self-destructive tendencies and replace them with positivity for the new beginning.

Archangel Gabriel enhances your spiritual awareness.

https://commons.wikimedia.org/wiki/File:Archangel_Gabriel;_The_Virgin_Annunciate_MET_ep1975.1.120c.bw.R.jpg

Flowers, herbs, and trees corresponding to Gabriel are chamomile, houseleek, poppy, moonwort, evening primrose, aloe vera, purslane, passionflower, honesty, watercress, mallow, weeping willow, yellow flag, jasmine, sweet flag, water lily, white lily, comfrey, white rose, lemon balm, lotus, and white poppy.

In Tarot, Archangel Gabriel is associated with The Hanged Man and The Chariot. Both cards indicate that this angel has tremendous influence over destiny, which is also underlined in the Moon's influence on Gabriel's work and abilities. Gabriel can establish the flow of life, whether it's a child from conception to early childhood or finding your purpose and direction in life. Gabriel's connection to the hanged man also alludes to the possible connection to higher spiritual knowledge and psychic abilities.

Other Associations:

Hours of the day and night:

- The 4th and 11th hours of the day and the 6th hour of the night on Sunday.
- The 1st and 8th hours of the day and the 3rd and 10th hours of the night on Monday.
- The 5th and 12th hours of the day and the 7th hour of the night on Tuesday.
- The 2nd and 9th hours of the day and the 4th and 11th hours of the night on Wednesday.
- The 6th hour of the day and the 1st and 8th hours of the night on Thursday.
- The 3rd and 10th hours of the day and the 5th and 12th hours of the night on Friday.
- The 7th hour of the day and the 2nd and 9th hours of the night on Saturday.

Element and mode: Water - Cardinal.

Season: Summer.

Month: January.

Metals: Silver and quicksilver.

Color: Amber and silver.

Crystals: Moonstone, turquoise, pearl, cat's eye, amber, opal, emerald.

Animals: Seagull, crab, turtle, sphinx.

Body part: Stomach, digestive tract, and breast area.

Incense: Jasmine, Onycha, and Myrrh.

Harmonious signs: Taurus, Scorpio, and Pisces.

Deities: Mercury, Apollo, and Khepera.

Ages ruled: 7 years.

Samael

Governing the planet Mars, Samael is associated with Tuesday. He is known for his righteous anger and ability to cleanse away negative influences. He can challenge you to prove that you are worthy of the sacred trust and shouldn't be summoned in inconsequential matters. He also bestows protection when you're feeling vulnerable and eliminates doubts and thoughts of weakness, replacing them with spiritual empowerment to stand against those who abuse power.

Flowers, herbs, and trees to use when working with Samael include gentian, geranium, thistle, gorse, snapdragon, hawthorn, common rue, High John the conqueror, gorse, pennyroyal, wormwood, tiger lily, cowslip, wild rose, chestnut, holly, pine, and sage.

In Tarot, Samael is linked to The Emperor and The Tower cards, which gives this angel an ambivalent quality. On the one hand, Samael is regarded as the angel and harbinger of death and is also said to be a magician. On the other hand, he hints at divine justice, an equally powerful male influence. Together, the two cards can put a lot of pressure on the angel and, in turn, on you.

Other Associations:

Hours of the day and night:

- The 7th hour of the day and the 2nd and 9th hours of the night on Sunday
- The 4th and 11th hours of the day and the 6th hour of the night on Monday
- The 1st and 8th hours of the day and the 3rd and 10th hours of the night on Tuesday

- The 5th and 12th hours of the day and the 7th hour of the night on Wednesday
- The 2nd and 9th hours of the day and the 4th and 11th hours of the night on Thursday
- The 6th hour of the day and the 1st and 8th hours of the night on Friday
- The 3rd and 10th hours of the day and the 5th and 12 hours of the night on Saturday

Element and mode: Fire - Cardinal.

Season: Spring.

Month: December.

Metals: Iron.

Color: Pink, red, white, and scarlet.

Crystals: Diamond, bloodstone, red jasper, ruby, and garnet.

Animals: Magpie, ram, owl, bull, and robin.

Body part: Face, neck, head, brain, and nervous system.

Incense: Dragons blood and allspice.

Harmonious Signs: Leo and Sagittarius.

Deities: Mars, Isis, Minerva, Athena, and Shiva.

Ages: 28-35 years.

Raphael

As the governor of Mercury, Raphael is linked to Wednesday. Due to the influence of this planet, Raphael is known for his protective and healing abilities. He can restore physical, emotional, or spiritual balance, chase away worrisome thoughts, and ground you to nature and the universe. Mercury is the planet of communication; through it, Raphael provides spiritual insights and lessens the negative impact of modern living on spiritual health.

Flowers, herbs, and trees to use to work with this Archangel are caraway, orchid, summer savory, clary sage, gladioli, pimpernel, clover, parsley, lily of the valley, lavender, dill, elecampane, iris, snapdragons, elder, mastic, sandalwood, jasmine, and lavender.

Corresponding to The Fool and The Lovers cards in Tarot, Raphael is the angel of wisdom, healing, and scientific discoveries. With this card,

Raphael can help you discover your true values and defend you against malicious influences. He can also teach you how to manifest your desires, end undesirable processes, or create challenges that will hone your skills and give you a chance to grow spiritually.

Other Correspondences:

Hours of the day and night:

- The 3rd and 10th hours of the day and the 5th and 12th hours of the night on Sunday.
- The 7th hour of the day and the 2nd and 9th hours of the night on Monday.
- The 4th and 11th hours of the day and the 6th hour of the night on Tuesday.
- The 1st and 8th hours of the day and the 3rd and 10th hours of the night on Wednesday.
- The 5th and 12th hours of the day and the 7th hour of the day on Thursday.
- The 2nd and 9th hours of the day and the 4th and 11th hours of the night on Friday.
- The 6th hour of the day and the 1st and 8th hours of the night on Saturday.

Element and mode: Air - Mutable.

Season: Winter - Spring.

Month: April.

Metals: Aluminum and quicksilver.

Color: Orange, white, and yellow.

Crystals: Yellow jasper, citrine, onyx, Iceland spar, topaz, diamond, jade, aquamarine, moss agate, and tourmaline.

Animals: Magpies, finches, and parrots.

Body part: Arms, lungs, and the respiratory system.

Incense: Wormwood, clover, and lavender.

Harmonious Signs: Libra and Aquarius.

Deities: Freya, Frey, Sekhmet, Janus, Bast, Pollux, and Castor.

Ages: 7-14 years.

Sachiel

Ruling over Jupiter, Sachiel is linked to Thursday. This indicates the angel's benevolent nature as he teaches that by giving back, you'll be able to meet your own needs much faster. He can also empower rituals designed to manifest abundant harvests, prosperity, the good of all, and physical and emotional security.

Some flowers, herbs, and trees corresponding to Sachiel are agrimony, wood betony, wood avens, valerian, borage, meadowsweet, cinquefoil, linden, dandelion, hyssop, honeysuckle, willow, heliotrope, elm, carnation, chicory, opium poppy, lilies, lilac, and sage.

In Tarot, Sachiel is paired with The Moon card, also governed by Jupiter. Through this card, the angel can bring you prestige, financial security, and social expansion. It's often a game changer in life and forces you to be patient to persevere in challenging times.

Other Correspondences:

Hours of the day and night:

- The 6th hour of the day and the 1st and 8th hours of the night on Sunday.
- The 3rd and 10th hours of the day and the 5th and 12th hours of the night on Monday.
- The 7th hour of the day and the 2nd and 9th hours of the night on Tuesday.
- The 4th and 11th hours of the day and the 6th hour of the night on Wednesday.
- The 1st and 8th hours of the day and the 3rd and 10th hours of the night on Thursday.
- The 5th and 12th hours of the day and the 7th hour of the night on Friday.
- The 2nd and 9th hours of the day and the 4th and 11th hours of the night on Saturday.

Element and mode: Water - Mutable.

Season: Winter.

Month: February.

Metals: Tin.

Color: Crimson blue, white, and purple.

Crystals: Lapis lazuli, pearl, turquoise, emerald, sapphire, and amethyst.

Animals: Ox, sheep, dolphin, stork, seal, and swan.

Body part: Circulatory system, lymphatic system, pineal glands, body fluids, toes, and feet.

Incense: Sage, ambergris, and sandalwood.

Harmonious Signs: Virgo, Cancer, and Scorpio.

Deities: Neptune, Anubis, Vishnu, Poseidon, and Khepera.

Ages: 55-62 years.

Anael

Governing Venus, Anael, has a strong connection to Friday. As one of the seven angels associated with creation, Anael is known for his pure, altruistic love. Influenced by Venus, Anael can teach you to love people and other beings around you and all creatures in the universe. He can inspire self-forgiveness and help you move on. At the same time, Venus is associated with fertility. Anael can then restore natural balance and help nature thrive.

Archangel Anael symbolizes love.

https://commons.wikimedia.org/wiki/File:Anael_como_el_regente_de_la_Luna.jpg

Flowers, herbs, and trees you can use when working with aneal are almond, aloe vera, violet, apple, calendula, tansy, cherry, rose, cornflower, pansy, cowslip, myrtle, crocus, marshmallow, feverfew, lady's mantle, iris, geranium, heather, goldenrod, walnut, and plum.

In Tarot, Anael is linked to the cards Hierophant and Justice, which influence love, nurturing feelings, children, knowledge, inner power, moral values, and inner self. The two cards help this angel give people hints on the adequate emotional perspective they need in relationships.

Other Correspondences:

Hours of the day and night:

- The 2nd and 9th hours of the day and the 4th and 11th hours of the night on Sunday.
- The 6th hour of the day and the 1st and 8th hours of the night on Monday.
- The 3rd and 10th hours of the day and the 5th and 12th hours of the night on Tuesday.
- The 7th hour of the day and the 2nd and 9th hours of the night on Wednesday.
- The 4th and 11th hours of the day and the 6th hour of the night on Thursday.
- The 1st and 8th hours of the day and the 3rd and 10th hours of the night on Friday.
- The 5th and 12th hours of the day and the 7th hour of the night on Saturday.

Element and mode: Air - Cardinal.

Season: Winter.

Month: December.

Metals: Copper.

Color: Black, emerald green, and royal blue.

Crystals: Lapis lazuli, jade, opal, chrysolite, emerald, and beryl.

Animals: Hare, dove, swan, sparrow, tortoise, and elephant.

Body part: Kidney, lower back, and liver.

Incense: Galbanum.

Season: Winter.

Deities: Vulcan, Ma, Maat, Yama, and Themis.

Ages: 14-21 years.

Cassiel

Cassiel is the Archangel associated with Saturn and Saturday. This alludes to Cassiel's ability as the conservator of strengths and ruler of temperance and solitude. Saturn has great power over investment opportunities. The planet helps the angel bring moderation into people's actions and pushes them to develop patience and the aptitude for contemplation. Cassiel can help reverse bad fortune and conserve your resources in trying times.

Flowers, herbs, and trees corresponding to Cassiel are aconite, skullcap, belladonna, poison hemlock, black nightshade, mullein, bluebell, mandrake, comfrey, henbane, foxglove, hellebore, fumitory, thyme, cypress, and pine.

In Tarot, Cassiel is associated with The World card, indicating power over property, home, and land, but also showing concern over poverty, old age, and long-term illnesses. Cassiel can teach you that you can only receive certain blessings later in life, so you'll have something to look forward to after many years of hard work.

Other Correspondences:

Hours of the day and night:

- The 5th and 12th hours of the day and the 7th hour of the night on Sunday
- The 2nd and 9th hours of the day and the 4th and 11th hours of the night on Monday
- The 6th hour of the day and the 1st and 8th hours of the night on Tuesday
- The 3rd and 10th hours of the day and the 5th and 12th hours of the night on Wednesday
- The 7th hour of the day and the 2nd and 9th hours of the night on Thursday
- The 4th and 11th hours of the day and the 6th hour of the night on Friday
- The 1st and 8th hours of the day and the 3rd and 10th hours of the night on Saturday

Element and mode: Air-Fixed.

Season: Winter.

Month: July.

Metals: Lead and aluminum.

Color: Purple, violet, and sky blue.

Crystals: Malachite, amber, lapis lazuli, aquamarine, garnet, obsidian, and jet.

Animals: Otter, eagle, peacock, and dog.

Body part: Ankles and the circulatory system.

Incense: Galbanum.

Harmonious sign: Leo.

Deities: Juno, Athena, and Nuit.

Ages: 49-56 years.

Angels Associated with the Seasons

Spring

Angels linked to spring are Spugliguel, Amatiel, Milkiel, Core, Carascara, and Commissoros. Milkiel provides the nurturing energy that brings about spring, then Spugliguel takes over as its guardian. The other angels represent rebirth and rejuvenation, creativity, and fun. They can also help plant ideas and establish communication, friendships, and sexual relationships. Spring-ruling angels are also associated with healing, purification, financial matters, harvest, fertility, air, and pastel colors.

Summer

Summer is primarily ruled by Tubiel. Gargatel, Tariel, and Gaviel are also linked to this season. Tubiel is the guardian of small birds and helps them return to their owners. The other angels rule over the Summer, allowing for exponential growth in nature and life. They can help you get inspired with ideas for projects, deepen your relationship or obtain the wealth and wisdom of the universe. They can also nudge you toward the path of love, strength, and partnership. Summer-ruling angels are associated with the fire element and the colors yellow, blue, pink, and green.

Autumn

Torquaret is the angel governing the season, with the angels Guabarel and Tarquam acting as its guardians. Just like the season to which they're linked, these angels rule over harvest, planning for winter months and bringing processes to an end. They can help you sort out ownership over possessions, find new things to study and heal from past traumas. Autumn governing angels are associated with the water elements and the colors orange, yellow, brown, tan, and brown.

Winter

The ruler of the winter season is Attaris, but the angels Cetarari, Amabael, and Archangel Michael also help out. The latter is associated with the snow, while the others ensure rest and relaxation. They can help you lay plans for the following spring, nourish your body, mind, and soul, go over your accomplishments, and find creativity during the coldest season. Winter ruling angels are associated with breaking negative habits, the earth element, magic, and the colors gray, white, red, and green.

Chapter 8: The Law of Attraction

Positivity attracts positive energy, and negativity attracts negative energy. You bring into your life what you send out to the world.

Oprah Winfrey said she used to visualize herself as a successful woman who could make a difference in the world. Jim Carrey also said that before he was famous, he wrote himself a cheque for ten million dollars and dated it Thanksgiving 1995. He expected that he would make this amount of money in five years. Interestingly, in 1995, before Thanksgiving, Jim Carrey's movie Dumb and Dumber was a huge success, and he made ten million dollars.

Oprah Winfrey and Jim Carrey made their dreams a reality with hard work and perseverance. However, the power of belief gave them the push and put them on the right track. They believed that they could, and they did. That was the Law of Attraction at work.

What Is the Law of Attraction?

The law of attraction is one of the seven universal laws, and it is a philosophy that focuses on the power of thought and its impact on people's lives. It suggests that positive thoughts bring good experiences and positive influences, while negative ones attract negativity and bring negative outcomes into people's lives. According to this notion, thoughts are made of vibrational frequencies. If they give off the right frequency, your thoughts are positive, and you will attract good things in your life, like success, happiness, strong relationships, money, and good health. This makes your thoughts extremely powerful since they can influence every area of your life.

Buddha believed that people become what they think.

https://pixabay.com/es/illustrations/buda-zen-meditaci%C3%B3n-4264589/

Buddha believed that people become their thoughts, attracting what they feel and creating what they imagine. Ancient Chinese philosopher Lao Tzu also stressed the significance of thoughts. He said that one should always be aware of them since they become words that eventually influence your actions. Your actions will then become habits that impact your character and who you want to be. Your character will become your future and your destiny. Basically, who you become starts with one thought.

For instance, if you want to lose weight, you must transform your thoughts and believe that you can change your lifestyle, eat healthily, and visualize yourself in perfect shape. This mindset will keep you going, and the positivity will attract more positive changes in your life.

- Your thoughts will focus on losing weight
- You will then tell yourself that you can do it
- This will influence your actions, and you will start working out and eating more healthily
- This lifestyle will become a habit that influences your character, and you will be a fit and healthy person

However, if you keep telling yourself that you won't lose weight, these thoughts will prevent you from taking action, as the negativity will hold you back.

You are like a magnet that is constantly attracting energies and thoughts. Whether you believe in the law of attraction or not, it still governs your life. Similar to gravity, the law of attraction applies to everyone. It doesn't just favor the people who believe in it; it is a fact and one of the strongest powers in the universe.

However, there are many misconceptions about the law of attraction. The most common one is that people often treat it like Aladdin's genie and expect it to make their wishes come true. They think the universe will only give them what they want if they think hard about it. For instance, some people believe that if you think about owning a big house, the universe will give it to you. This isn't how this law works. It requires positive thinking, believing you deserve what you want, and working hard for it. As a result, the universe will open doors for you and provide you with opportunities until you achieve your goals. In other words, just like your thoughts, action is a big part of the law of attraction.

Some people prefer to keep their hopes and dreams to themselves because, deep down, they believe they won't accomplish them. They surrender to the darkness and think they aren't smart, strong, or talented enough to get what they want. If you don't feel comfortable sharing your dreams with others, communicate them to the universe instead. Spread them out with positive energy, and be ready to receive all the blessings you ever wanted.

The law of attraction works using manifestation. Raise your energy and keep it high for as long as you can. Understandably, one can't always be expected to think positively; this isn't realistic. Life can be stressful, and you're bound to encounter things that can upset you or ruin your mood. The point is to keep negative thoughts out of your head and focus on your goal and the life you want to build for yourself.

The History of the Law of Attraction

In 2006, when "The Secret" by Rhonda Byrne was published, everyone was talking about the law of attraction, so it is easy to assume that it is a modern notion. However, it has been around for almost two centuries. Russian author Helena Blavatsky was the first person to coin the phrase "law of attraction" in 1877 in her book "The Secret Doctrine." Although she didn't delve into details or provide any significant information, she introduced the concept and laid the foundation on which many other authors based their work. Helena mentioned that people and their abilities are defined by their thoughts and that they are so powerful that they can shape one's reality. American author Prentice Mulford was the first person to introduce it as a universal law.

In 1907, American author William Walker Atkinson provided more information about the law of attraction in his book "Thinking Vibration or the Law of Attraction in the Thought World." The book was a great success, and many found it very interesting. It was a great inspiration to modern scholars who based their work on Atkinson's writing. He mentioned the concept of vibration in his book, which wasn't popular at the time. He also discussed other notions as well like manifestation, energy, and the principles of thinking.

After Atkinson's work became popular, other writers were fascinated with the concept. In 1910, American writer Wallace Delois Wattles discussed the law of attraction in his book "The Science of Getting Rich." He stressed the idea of the value of thinking in the process of manifestation. He also noted that everything in the universe is made up of energy.

In 1928, American author Napoleon Hill released the book "The Law of Success in 16 Lessons." Hill mentioned the phrase "the law of attraction" multiple times in his book and introduced the concept to a wider audience. In 1986, American author Esther Hicks and her husband, Jerry Hicks, published the insightful book "The Law of Attraction."

However, in 2006, the law of attraction turned from a fascinating concept that authors and philosophers studied and wrote about to a worldwide phenomenon. One can't deny the great contribution Jerry and Esther Hicks made. However, there were people who were skeptical. Although the book was successful among philosophers and scholars, it failed to achieve commercial success.

This all changed with the release of "The Secret." Everyone became curious about the law of attraction and wanted to learn about it. After the book's success, Byrne released a documentary about "The Secret," in which philosophers, authors, and scientists discussed the law of attraction and its meaning. Like the book, the movie was a great success, and millions of people worldwide were interested in and talking about the law of attraction.

Byrne stated in "The Secret" that your thoughts could create anything, you can only succeed if you believe in yourself, and you can manifest your goals with positive thoughts and emotions.

Although the law of attraction was first coined in the 1800s, ancient philosophers like Buddha and Tzu mentioned the idea behind it in many of their writings.

The Principles of the Law of Attraction

One can only understand the law of attraction by learning about its main principles.

Like Attracts Like

Unlike the popular belief that opposites attract, the law of attraction introduces a different theory that like attracts like. That basically means that you attract thoughts similar to yours. This also applies to people. Look at your circle of friends, and you will notice that you often gravitate toward people like you. It is human nature to prefer to surround yourself with people with whom you share common interests and personality traits.

You never have just one negative thought. Once your mind begins thinking negatively, it alters your thought patterns and changes your perspective. For instance, you gain weight and convince yourself that you will never be able to lose it and get in shape. This thought will attract others like "I hate myself," "I am ugly," "no one will love me," "I have never been able to lose weight because I am a failure," etc.

You can only get over the ideas that hold you back by releasing them and replacing them with positive ones. Understand that these negative thoughts aren't realistic or rational. They are just a reflection of your fears and insecurities, but if you face them and apply logical thinking, you will see that they don't hold any merit.

Interestingly, if there is something you lack, you will attract more of that emptiness. For instance, if you are in debt, you will attract more debt. Similarly, you also attract what you don't need. For instance, if you have a job that you are comfortable in, you will be more likely to receive other job offers.

Nature Abhors Clutter

When your brain is cluttered with negative thoughts, there won't be any room for positivity in your life. Eliminate the negativity to free up space to attract positive thoughts and good experiences. If your home is cluttered with things you don't need, it will impact your mental health, and you won't have any room for newer or nicer stuff. Remember, if your brain is cluttered, so will every aspect of your life.

The Present Isn't Always Perfect

Life isn't always easy, and for most people, the present is anything but perfect. There are always wars, diseases, and people dying, besides the stresses you face on a daily basis. Whether it is relationship troubles or a job that sucks the life out of you, there are things that can make it hard to see the good in life.

Most people don't live in the moment. They either let their brains wander to the past and live in regret or are constantly worried about the future. However, there is no point since the past is already gone, and there is nothing you can do to change it, and the future isn't guaranteed. Focus on the present and work on making it perfect.

This point emphasizes that there are always things in the present that can stress you out and make you unhappy. Don't spend your time focusing on the bad things. Instead, improve them and make things easier for yourself. This is better than spending your energy on being miserable and helpless. There will be times when you feel sad, and negative thoughts will definitely creep in at some point, but you are allowed to feel and acknowledge them. Fix what you can, and don't dwell on the things that are out of your control.

Say you are stuck in a dead-end job with a boss who is making your life hard. You can either spend your time complaining or find ways to fix the situation. Either keep sending out resumes while believing that you will find another job or work harder at your current one and better yourself by learning new skills.

Don't waste your energy complaining about your job or boss to your friends and family. Instead, visualize the job of your dreams and talk about it with your loved ones, and you will attract it into your life.

Universal Law

The law of attraction resembles the concept of karma; what goes around comes around. You not only get back the thoughts you release to the universe but also all the good deeds you do. The way you treat others will directly influence your life. Kindness and love attract positive emotions, and people will treat you the same way you treat them. For instance, if you smile at someone, they will smile back at you. When you treat the people below you at work with respect, they will admire and look up to you. However, if you hurt, disrespect, or offend someone, they will respond similarly to you.

Always help those in need; whenever you are in trouble, the universe will send you someone to lend you a helping hand.

Harmony

Your surroundings have a huge impact on your energy. They can influence your thoughts and change your outlook on life. Stay in a positive environment and surround yourself with people who lift you up and influence your thoughts.

Now that you understand the law of attraction and the impact it can have on your life, certain exercises can help you.

Meditation Technique

Instructions:

1. Find a quiet room with no distractions.
2. Sit in a comfortable position.
3. Close your eyes and take a few deep breaths.
4. Focus on the recurring patterns in your life. Spend a few minutes observing them and how often you react to them.
5. Next, turn your attention to the negative thoughts or emotions that result from the recurring themes.
6. Understand the way you deal with these patterns and interpret your life along with the beliefs you hold dear.
7. Ask your higher self to guide you so you can see if your actions are influencing your current situation.
8. Focus your attention on one significant pattern and contemplate all the times its theme was present in your life. Ask yourself what was going on in your life at the time and what your environment looked like?
9. Ponder on your mindset during that time. What were your thoughts and beliefs? How did you feel as a result of your situation? How did your energy and internal reality impact the energy you attracted and the reality you created?
10. How did you express yourself at the time? How did you react to your surroundings and the situation you were facing? How did this pattern end? Were you the one who ended it, or was it an external factor?

11. What lessons did you learn from this experience, and how did you react to them? Did the experience make you any wiser? How can these lessons activate the law of attraction so you can attract positive thoughts, emotions, and experiences in the future?
12. Next, set an intention that you want to heal all the wounds and let go of the old beliefs from your past that have contributed to the negativity. You can say something like, *"I am healing my wounds and releasing my past beliefs and mistakes to free space for love and positivity to enter my life. I am letting go of all the thoughts and emotions that no longer serve me."*
13. Imagine your guardian angel sending you healing energy and love to heal all your wounds.
14. Feel the healing energy flowing through every part of you and invite the pattern, belief, or person from which you want to heal to appear before you. Now, transfer this energy from your heart to them with the intention of healing their wounds as well.
15. Express your feelings while transferring your energy and ask your higher self for guidance.
16. Now, with love, cut the energetic chord connecting you with the situation or being and watch it as it dissolves.
17. Focus on what energy, thoughts, or emotions you want to manifest or bring into your life right now.
18. Imagine the energy or thoughts as a bright, colorful light bringing you joy, comfort, and excitement. Believe that you are already experiencing these feelings, and notice how your mood will change for the better.
19. Take in everything around you, like the sounds, scents, or feelings, while keeping your eyes closed.
20. Feel the positive thoughts and emotions flowing through you.
21. Express your gratitude for all the blessings the universe has given you.
22. Take a deep breath when the image you created in your imagination looks and feels real.

23. Breathe out while imagining giving energy to your visualization. The air you exhale will give it power and life.
24. Sit with this image for a few minutes and feel how your thoughts and emotions change.
25. After you finish and feel ready to return to the real world, take a long deep breath, release it, and slowly open your eyes.

Visualization

Instructions:

1. Lie in bed and get comfortable.
2. Close your eyes, clear your mind, and relax your body.
3. Feel the mattress against your skin and take in the scent of the room.
4. Focus on the sounds around you, like birds chirping outside, your partner's breathing next to you, or the sound of the wind.
5. Now, visualize all the things you want to attract into your life.

Vision Board

Tools:

- A flat surface
- Objects that represent your goals, like quotes, words, or photos
- Scissors
- Clips or glue
- Printer

Instructions:

1. Set an intention that you want to create a vision board to activate the law of attraction to bring a certain dream into your life, like love or a better career.
2. Set a time frame for the board. This will depend on the goal. For instance, if your goal is to be promoted, the time frame can be one or two years.
3. Decide on the type of vision board you want to create, like a wall grid or a collage. Choose whatever makes you feel happy and comfortable.

4. Prepare your supplies and choose things that motivate you, inspire you, and fill you with positivity whenever you look at them.
5. Create the vision board by pasting the images and quotes together on a collage. You can even write down the quotes or draw the images.
6. After creating the vision board, place it in a location you see every day.

Tips:

- Remember that the law of attraction is all about positivity, so it won't recognize negative statements like "I don't want to be sick anymore," the board will interpret that as "I want to get sick." Keep your words and tone positive. The images and quotes you choose should also be cheerful to attract similar thoughts into your life.
- Choose your words carefully. Don't say, "I want to heal from my sickness," because your energy will focus on the word "sickness." You can say, "I want to heal and be strong and healthy."
- Speak about your goals as if you have already achieved them.

You are what you think, so be aware of where your mind wanders. Remember to remain in the present since it is guaranteed, the future is unknown, and the past isn't relevant anymore.

Although you can't always control negative thoughts, try to be aware of them. Don't fight them. Acknowledge them when they occur, then let them go. Understand that you are stronger than these thoughts and that you have the power to release them.

The law of attraction has been around since the beginning of time. It teaches mankind the significance of thoughts and that you receive what you send to the universe. Keep your thoughts positive and let go of all the negativity impacting your life. Use positive statements when you talk about yourself and your goals. Believe that you can achieve everything you set your mind to and that the universe is guiding you.

Chapter 9: Daily Meditations

Have you ever found yourself bewildered by the seemingly cryptic signs that the universe seems to be throwing your way? Perhaps you've come across repeating number patterns, such as 111 or 333, and been intrigued about their significance? It's all too common to feel disoriented and uncertain when attempting to decipher these messages. But don't worry! Meditation is here to serve as your beacon.

Daily meditation is the key to self-awareness and connecting with your inner self.

This chapter will unveil meditation's profound role in forging an intimate connection with your inner self, fostering emotional stability, and cultivating heightened self-awareness. By delving into specialized exercises, you'll learn how to awaken your third eye chakra, thus demystifying the obscured meanings encoded within those enigmatic angel numbers.

So, if you are in pursuit of understanding and guidance, take a deep breath, let go of any tension, and prepare to embark on a journey of exploration into how meditation can equip you with the keys to unlocking the cosmic code of the universe.

Enhancing Awareness

Cultivating mindfulness carries many advantages, spanning from sharpening focus to mitigating stress and anxiety, all while bolstering overall wellness. In this section, you will find a variety of exercises and meditation practices designed to amplify your consciousness. These will serve as your road map on the exciting expedition towards elevated self-awareness.

- **Mindful Breathing Exercise**

Sit comfortably in a chair or cross-legged on a cushion. Close your eyes and focus on your breath. Inhale deeply through your nose and feel your lungs filling up. Slowly exhale, feeling your stomach deflate.

Continue deep breathing for a few minutes, paying attention to the sensation of the air moving in and out of your body. Every time your mind wanders, bring your attention back to your breath. You can repeat this exercise as many times throughout the day as needed, even if just for a few minutes.

- **Body Scan Meditation**

Lie down in a comfortable position and close your eyes. Slowly scan your body, starting from the top of your head and moving down to your toes. As you focus on each body part, visualize releasing any tension or tightness present. Relax and take deep breaths.

Begin with the crown chakra and focus on that area for a moment before slowly making your way down the other chakras throughout the central line of your body – brow, throat, heart, solar plexus, sacral, and root. Stay with each chakra for a moment and notice what it feels like as you inhale and exhale.

- **Mindful Eating Exercise**

Enjoy a meal or snack in a relaxed environment with minimal distractions. As you eat, pay attention to each bite's texture, flavor, and temperature in your mouth. Notice how the food makes you feel. Mindful eating can help with overindulgent behavior.

- **Walking Meditation**

Find a quiet place to walk, like a garden or a park. Walk slowly and focus on each step, noticing how your feet contact the ground. Focus your mind on your breath to stay present in the moment. You can even take this walking meditation to hallways or paths around your home or workplace, taking a few minutes for yourself to feel the peace moving and breathing bring.

- **Gratitude Meditation**

Sit comfortably and focus on the things or people you appreciate. Begin by taking time to visualize everything you have to be grateful for, from the small things, like a warm cup of coffee, to more significant things, like the people in your life. Try focusing your attention on how these elements make you feel.

Finally, take a few deep breaths, and imagine yourself extending gratitude to the source of these positive experiences. This can be a religious or spiritual figure, the universe, or even a person you are thanking directly.

- **Yoga**

There are numerous yoga styles - beginners may find starting with a restorative practice to be the most approachable. Yoga focuses on bringing awareness to your breath and body, allowing you to relax and center yourself.

These exercises and meditations are just a few examples of how you can focus on increasing awareness. Starting with just one practice and building on it over time can lead to noticeable benefits. With enough patience and dedication, you will improve your focus, reduce anxiety, and live life to the fullest.

Connecting to the Angelic Realm

Connecting to the angelic realm through meditation can be a powerful and transformative experience. This spiritual practice can help you tap into higher consciousness, gain clarity and insight, and feel a deeper connection to the divine.

1. To start, find a quiet, comfortable space where you won't be disturbed. Take a few deep breaths to settle into your body and release any tension or stress. Close your eyes and focus your attention on your breath, feeling the sensation of the air moving in and out of your body.
2. As you continue to breathe deeply, visualize a bright light surrounding you. This light represents the divine energy that surrounds and protects you. Allow yourself to feel the warmth and love of this light, and let it fill your entire being.
3. Next, imagine a staircase in front of you, leading up into the clouds. This is your gateway to the angelic realm. As you ascend the stairs, feel yourself becoming lighter and more peaceful. With each step, you are moving closer to the divine realm.
4. When you reach the top of the stairs, imagine standing in a beautiful garden filled with flowers, trees, and animals. This is the place where angels and other divine beings reside. Take a moment to look around. Noticing the colors, scents, and sounds of this sacred space.
5. As you continue to breathe deeply, call forth the presence of your guardian angel. Ask for their guidance, love, and support as you connect with the angelic realm. You may feel a warm sensation, a tingling, or a sense of peace as you connect with your angel.
6. Take some time to chat with your angel, asking any questions on your mind. Listen to their voice, which may come to you as a feeling, a thought, or a vision. Trust that they are communicating with you *in the best way for you.*
7. As you connect with your angelic guides, feel yourself becoming more attuned to your intuition and your inner wisdom. Allow yourself to receive any insights or messages that come to you. Know that you are supported and guided by the divine forces.
8. When you feel ready, thank your angels for their guidance and love. Visualize yourself going down the staircase back to

the physical realm, feeling grounded and centered. Take a few more deep breaths before opening your eyes.

To deepen your connection with the angelic realm, you may want to consider making meditation a regular practice. Set aside a few minutes daily to connect with your angels and tune into your inner guidance. Over time, you may find that this practice helps you live a more joyful, peaceful, and fulfilling life.

Mediation for Opening Third Eye Chakra

Meditation is a powerful tool for opening the third eye or crown chakra. The third eye chakra is located between the eyebrows and is associated with intuition, spiritual awareness, and psychic abilities. On the other hand, the crown chakra is located at the top of the head and is associated with divine wisdom, unity, and consciousness. Opening these chakras can enhance your spiritual connection with the universe and help you attain a deep sense of inner peace and fulfillment.

1. To begin, find a quiet, peaceful space where you will not be disturbed. You can sit cross-legged on a mat or pillow.
2. Make sure your back is straight and your shoulders are relaxed. You can also choose to sit on a chair, but ensure your feet are planted firmly on the ground. Take a few deep breaths and feel the tension in your body going away as you exhale.
3. Close your eyes and visualize a bright light on your forehead. This light represents your third eye chakra.
4. Focus on this light and imagine it expanding and growing in intensity. Visualize the light shining down and piercing through any blockages or obstacles hindering the awakening of your third eye chakra.
5. As you continue to focus on your third eye chakra, begin to breathe slowly and deeply. Inhale through your nose, hold your breath for a few seconds, and then exhale through your mouth.
6. As you breathe, feel the energy flowing through your body and visualize it reaching your third eye chakra. As you continue to breathe, shift your focus to your crown chakra. Visualize a bright white light at the top of your head. This

light represents your crown chakra. Imagine the light growing and expanding, filling your entire body with divine wisdom and spiritual connection.

7. Now, focus on both your third eye chakra and your crown chakra simultaneously. Visualize the energy flowing freely between these two chakras. Imagine the bright light at your third eye chakra merging with the bright white light at your crown chakra, creating a powerful connection between your spiritual and intuitive self.
8. As you continue to meditate, try to maintain this visualization for at least 10-15 minutes. If your mind wanders, gently bring your focus back to your breath and chakras. You can also incorporate affirmations, such as *"I am connected to my intuition and my divine self"* or *"I trust in the universe to guide me on my path."*

After your meditation, take a few moments to sit with your eyes closed and feel the energy in your body. Visualize the bright light at your third eye chakra and your crown chakra continuing to glow brightly, even as you go about your day.

Opening your third eye or crown chakra through meditation can enhance your spiritual growth and lead to a deeper sense of inner peace and fulfillment. You can awaken these chakras with consistent practice and cultivate a strong connection with your divine self.

Exercises to Open Third Eye Chakra

Opening your third eye or crown chakra can be a transformative experience that can help you tap into your intuition, enhance your spiritual practice, and improve your overall well-being. However, it can also be daunting to undertake such an exercise without proper guidance. Here is how you can open your third eye or crown chakra.

Step 1: Set the Intention

Start by setting the intention to open your third eye or crown chakra. To do this, sit in a quiet and comfortable space where you will not be disturbed. Close your eyes and take a few deep breaths. Imagine yourself surrounded by warm, peaceful, and protective energy. Then, internalize the intention to open your third eye or crown chakra. Repeat to yourself, "I am open and ready to receive universal energy and wisdom."

Step 2: Meditative Breathing

Next, begin with meditative breathing, also known as pranayama. There are many variations of pranayama, but one of the most commonly used techniques is the 4-7-8 breathing method. With this technique, you inhale for four seconds, hold your breath for seven seconds, and exhale for eight seconds. Repeat this for at least five minutes, and focus all of your awareness on your breathing. This will quiet your mind and prepare you for the next step.

Step 3: The Om Chant

The next step is to perform the Om chant. This powerful mantra can activate your third eye and crown chakra. Begin by taking a deep breath, and as you exhale, say the word Om. Repeat this several times, each time visualizing the sound filling your body and mind with positive energy.

Step 4: Forehead Massage

After chanting the Om mantra, gently massage your forehead with your fingers. Place your index and middle fingers between your eyebrows and apply gentle pressure in a circular motion. This will create a sense of warmth and release tension in this area.

Step 5: Visualization

Visualize a bright light in the forehead area. Picture this light expanding with each inhale and contracting with each exhale. Focus all of your attention on this visualization, allowing it to become more vivid and clearer with each breath.

Step 6: Crown Chakra Activation

Place your hands on the crown of your head, and visualize the top of your skull opening up. Picture a bright light shining down on your body and illuminating every cell. Feel this light penetrating your body with warmth, love, and wisdom.

Grounding and Cleansing Mediation

Mediation is a powerful practice that can help you ground yourself and cleanse your energy. It allows you to connect with your inner self and tap into your intuition while also helping you to release any negative or stagnant energy that may be holding you back. To get the most out of your mediation practice, it is important to follow these step-by-step instructions:

Step 1: Find a Quiet Space

The first step in any meditation practice is to find a quiet space to be alone and free from distractions. This could be a dedicated meditation space or a peaceful corner in your bedroom or living room.

Step 2: Set Your Intention

Once you have found your quiet space, take a few moments to set your intention for your meditation practice. This could be a simple goal, such as grounding yourself and clearing your energy, or it could be a more specific intention, such as connecting with your higher self or finding clarity on a specific issue.

Step 3: Get into a Comfortable Position

Next, get into a comfortable position, such as sitting cross-legged on the floor or lying down. Choosing a position that allows you to relax and be comfortable for the duration of your mediation practice is important.

Step 4: Focus on Your Breath

With your eyes closed, begin to focus on your breath. Take a deep inhale through your nose, filling your lungs with air, and then exhale slowly through your mouth. Repeat this deep breathing pattern for several minutes, allowing your body to become more relaxed with each breath.

Step 5: Visualize Roots Growing from Your Feet

To ground yourself, visualize roots growing from your feet and sinking deep into the earth below you. Imagine these roots anchoring you to the ground and providing a sense of stability and security. Take a few moments to focus on this visualization, allowing it to become more vivid in your mind's eye.

Step 6: Scan Your Body for Tension

As you continue to breathe deeply and focus on grounding yourself, scan your body for any areas of tension or discomfort. If you notice any tightness or discomfort, take a few moments to breathe into those areas and release the tension.

Step 7: Visualize a White Light

To cleanse your energy, visualize a bright white light flowing down from the universe and surrounding your body. See this light penetrating every cell and filling you with positive energy and light. As you continue to focus on this visualization, feel yourself becoming lighter and more energized.

Step 8: Release Any Negative Energy

As you visualize the white light surrounding your body, focus on releasing any negative or stagnant energy that may be weighing you down. Imagine it leaving your body and being carried away by the universe, leaving you feeling refreshed and rejuvenated.

Step 9: End with Gratitude

Finally, end your mediation practice by expressing gratitude for the experience. Take a few moments to reflect on how you feel and how your energy has shifted. Express gratitude for your body, mind, and spirit and for the countless blessings in your life.

Mediation is a powerful tool that can help you ground yourself and cleanse your energy. By following these step-by-step instructions, you can create a safe and nurturing space for yourself and tap into the infinite wisdom and energy of the universe. Whether you practice meditation daily or just occasionally, you are sure to experience the profound benefits of this ancient practice. So, take a deep breath, center yourself, and let the magic of meditation transform your life!

Uncovering Synchronicities in the Past

Mediation for uncovering synchronicities in the past can be a powerful tool for finding connections you may have previously overlooked. By meditating on your past experiences and actively seeking out synchronicities, you can gain insight into your innermost thoughts and feelings and ultimately achieve greater self-awareness.

Step 1: Set the Intention

The first step in mediating synchronicities is to set the intention to uncover them. This can involve verbalizing your desire to connect with the universe and gain insight into your past experiences. It is important to approach this process with an open mind and a willingness to be vulnerable.

Step 2: Connect with Your Breath

Once you have set your intention, it is time to begin the meditation process. Start by focusing on your breath and taking slow, deliberate breaths. This can calm your mind and center yourself, allowing you to better connect with your inner thoughts and feelings.

Step 3: Reflect on Your Past

Once you are calm and centered, begin reflecting on your past experiences. Think about significant events or moments in your life that have profoundly impacted you. Try to recall the emotions you felt during these events and any thoughts or beliefs you may have held at the time.

Step 4: Look for Patterns and Connections

As you reflect on your past experiences, start to look for patterns and connections between seemingly unrelated events. Pay attention to any recurring themes or symbols that emerge and any significant coincidences or synchronicities that may have occurred. Write these down in a journal or notebook to help you better analyze and understand these connections later.

Step 5: Interpret the Meaning

Once you have identified these patterns and connections, it is time to interpret their meaning. This can involve exploring your own subconscious thoughts and feelings, as well as seeking out guidance from spiritual sources or professionals. It is important to approach this process with an open mind and a willingness to explore new perspectives and ideas.

Step 6: Take Action

The final step in meditating for synchronicities is to take action based on the insights you have gained. This can involve making changes to your behavior, taking steps towards achieving a specific goal, or simply embracing a new outlook on life. By taking action, you can bring these synchronicities into your conscious awareness and use them as a guide to living a more purposeful and fulfilling life.

Meditating on Angel Symbols or Numbers

One way to practice meditation is by meditating on angel symbols or numbers. Here is how to meditate on angel symbols or numbers.

Step 1: Find a Quiet and Peaceful Place to Meditate

Find a quiet and peaceful place in your home where you can meditate without being disturbed. It could be a room, a corner, or even a specific chair. Make sure that the place is clean, well-ventilated, and comfortable.

Step 2: Use Angel Symbols or Numbers as Your Focus Point

Choose an angel symbol or number that resonates with you. There are different angel symbols and numbers which represent different meanings. For instance, the number 1111 can represent spiritual awakening, while Archangel Michael's symbol represents protection and courage. You can find different angel symbols and their meanings online or in books.

Step 3: Set Your Intention

Before you start meditating, set your intention. Decide what you want to achieve from this meditation. Your intention could be to connect with your guardian angel, receive guidance, or simply relax.

Step 4: Sit Comfortably

Sit in a comfortable position with your back straight. You can sit on a chair or the floor, whichever is more comfortable for you. Rest your hands on your lap, with your palms facing upwards.

Step 5: Close Your Eyes

Close your eyes and take a deep breath. Inhale and then exhale slowly. Repeat this a few times until you feel calm and relaxed.

Step 6: Visualize the Symbol or Number

Visualize the angel symbol or number in your mind's eye. Focus your attention on the symbol or number and allow it to fill your mind with positive energy. If you find it hard to visualize, you can also look at a picture of the angel symbol or number.

Step 7: Repeat a Mantra

Repeat a mantra or phrase corresponding to the angel symbol or number. For example, if you meditate on Archangel Michael's symbol, you can repeat the phrase "*I am safe and protected.*" Repeat the mantra or phrase in your mind or out loud as often as you want.

Step 8: Stay Focused

Stay focused on the symbol or number and your intention. If your mind wanders, gently bring your attention back to the symbol or number. Don't worry if you find it hard to stay focused at first; it takes practice.

Step 9: End the Meditation

End the meditation by taking a few deep breaths and gradually returning your awareness to your surroundings. Open your eyes and take a moment to stretch.

Step 10: Reflect on Your Experience

After the meditation, take a moment to reflect on your experience. Did you feel more relaxed? Were there any insights or messages that came to you? This reflection can help you gain more clarity on your intention and how you can improve.

Conclusion

If the angels try to send you a message, you'll suddenly start seeing the same sets of digits every time you look at the time, your bank statement, or an invoice. If you can spot angel numbers everywhere you go, this is a sign that you've been awakened by angels who wish to guide you toward the right path. Interpreting these messages can be challenging if your knowledge of angel numbers, numerology, and synchronicity is limited.

However, now that you've read this book, you should be able to understand the messages that the angels are sending you and know what to do about them. Reading this book should prepare you to work with angel symbolism and provide you with in-depth knowledge about various concepts related to angels and their connection to the universe. You'll find high-value information that you can use to transform your life and take the first steps toward personal growth and development.

This book explores the significance of angel numbers and numerology and how they're age-old spiritual practices. It explains the difference between divine timing, synchronicity, and coincidence and teaches you how to put the Law of Attraction to work. In the first few chapters, you learned about the origins, history, and basics of numerology and how angel numbers differ from other esoteric practices. Most importantly, you can now use your intuition and knowledge to analyze and address different number sequences and patterns.

Understanding the different ways in which angels communicate with people allows you to be more responsive to their messages and attempts to connect with you. With the right safety precautions in mind, you can engage in meditations and prayers that help you get in touch with your angels of choice and work with them to enhance certain aspects of your life.

If you know how to use it, you can use the Law of Attraction to drastically change your life. Understanding this phenomenon and learning about the philosophical and religious principles on which it is based can help you make the most out of using it. This book provides effective exercises and techniques you can use to activate the Law of Attraction.

The last chapter, which offers daily exercises and meditations that you can practice to enhance your awareness, connect to the angelic realm, and open your third eye and crown chakras, serves as a directory that you can always go back to at different points of your life. These practices can support your spiritual endeavors, improve your intuition, and make it easier to connect with the universe.

This book is the perfect opportunity for beginners and seasoned practitioners to enrich their spiritual practices and connect with the angelic realm. While it will take a lot of time, effort, dedication, and practice, reading this book has given you all the knowledge you need to transform your life and tip the universe in your favor.

This guide to angel numbers is an indispensable resource for anyone looking to expand their knowledge in the world of spiritual practices and improve their intuition. It offers a comprehensive understanding of key spiritual concepts that can help you unlock your full potential and lead a more fulfilling life.

Here's another book by Mari Silva that you might like

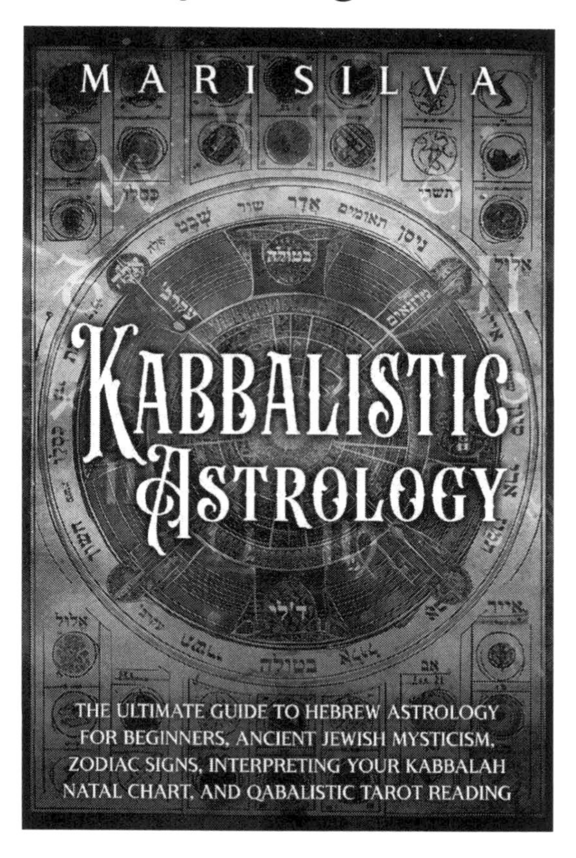

Your Free Gift
(only available for a limited time)

Thanks for getting this book! If you want to learn more about various spirituality topics, then join Mari Silva's community and get a free guided meditation MP3 for awakening your third eye. This guided meditation mp3 is designed to open and strengthen ones third eye so you can experience a higher state of consciousness. Simply visit the link below the image to get started.

https://spiritualityspot.com/meditation

References

- H. (2019, May 13). Being visited by Angels? Here are 14 Angel signs that you are! The Angel Writer. https://www.theangelwriter.com/blog/angel-signs

(N.d.-a). Psychicsource.com. https://www.psychicsource.com/numerology

(N.d.-b). T2conline.com. https://t2conline.com/the-history-of-numerology/

(N.d.-c). Instyle.com. https://www.instyle.com/lifestyle/astrology/numerology

12 signs an angel messenger is near - centre of excellence. (2019, March 18). Centreofexcellence.com. https://www.centreofexcellence.com/angel-messenger-12-signs/

18 signs you're experiencing A synchronicity (and not just coincidence). (2022, December 23). Mindbodygreen. https://www.mindbodygreen.com/articles/synchronicities

Allard, S. (2020, May 12). The beauty of synchronicity. Divineknowing.com. https://www.divineknowing.com/blog/the-beauty-of-synchronicity/

Angel Correspondences. (n.d.). Tripod.Com. https://athena523.tripod.com/angelcorres.htm

Angelic Correspondences in the Tarot. (2015, July 8). Angelorum. https://angelorum.co/topics/divination/angelic-messages-and-correspondences-in-the-tarot/

Angelic Correspondences. (1970, January 1). SpellsOfMagic. https://www.spellsofmagic.com/coven_ritual.html?ritual=152&coven=108

Archangelic Flower Correspondences. (2022, August 8). Angelorum. https://angelorum.co/angels-2/angel-mystic-monday/archangelic-flower-correspondences/

Aúgusta, J. (2023, February 17). Where can you see angel numbers? Ministry of Numerology. https://ministryofnumerology.com/where-can-you-see-angel-numbers/

Aymen. (2011, July 26). Angelic Correspondences. Spiritual.Com.Au. https://spiritual.com.au/2011/07/angelic-correspondences/

Beck, M. (2016, August 11). Martha beck: How to tell when the universe is sending you signs. Oprah.com. https://www.oprah.com/inspiration/martha-beck-how-to-tell-when-the-universe-is-sending-you-signs

Blair, S. (2022, May 30). What are angel numbers? A guide to the phenomenon and why it may occur. RUSSH; RUSSH Magazine. https://www.russh.com/what-are-angel-numbers/

Blanchard, T. (2021, December 3). 7 signs of divine timing working in your life. Outofstress.com. https://www.outofstress.com/signs-divine-timing-is-working/

Bose, S. D. (2022, September 8). When Jim Carrey wrote himself a $10 million cheque. Far Out Magazine. https://faroutmagazine.co.uk/jim-carrey-wrote-himself-10-million-cheque/

Bronzeman. (n.d.). Method of invoking angels, by Sigil Ritual proven to be effective. Opera.News. https://gh.opera.news/gh/en/religion/c9b4f2070eb6c478ad6dff37c26471fb

Canfield, J. (2021, September 8). A complete guide to using the law of Attraction. Jack Canfield. https://jackcanfield.com/blog/using-the-law-of-attraction/

Cheung, N. (2017, November 17). Signs of an angel watching over you. Woot & Hammy. https://wootandhammy.com/blogs/news/angel-signs-watching-over-you-guardian-angel-numbers

Debutify, & Tarot, A. (2021, August 3). What Are Angel Sigils? Apollo Tarot. https://apollotarot.com/blogs/insights/what-are-angel-sigils

Eatough, E. (n.d.). What is the law of attraction, and can you use it to change your life? Betterup.com. https://www.betterup.com/blog/what-is-law-of-attraction

Estrada, J. (2021, April 8). No, it's not just a coincidence—here's how to spot and decode spiritual synchronicities. Well+Good. https://www.wellandgood.com/what-does-synchronicity-mean-spiritually/

Glitch Digital. (2021, June 23). Jim carrey's law of attraction and visualization tips. Influencive. https://www.influencive.com/jim-carreys-law-of-attraction-and-visualization-tips/

Graf, S. (2012, July 15). How to meditate on the third eye for better intuition. WikiHow. https://www.wikihow.com/Meditate-on-the-Third-Eye

Günel, S. (2020, May 29). How to manifest your wildest dreams: A beginner's guide to the law of attraction. Mind Cafe. https://medium.com/mind-cafe/how-to-manifest-your-wildest-dreams-a-beginners-guide-to-the-law-of-attraction-b82ca96e7fc9

Henry Cornelius Agrippa. (n.d.). Umich.Edu. https://quod.lib.umich.edu/e/eebo/A26562.0001.001/1:13.19?rgn=div2;view=fulltext

History of Numerology – Kabbalah, Chaldean, Pythagorean, Chinese, Angelic Numerology. (2021, June 4). MyPandit. https://www.mypandit.com/numerology/history/

Hurst, K. (2019, June 5). Law Of Attraction history: Discovering the secret origins. The Law Of Attraction; Cosmic Media LLC. https://thelawofattraction.com/history-law-attraction-uncovered/

Hurst, K. (2023, March 7). 14 warning signs from angels - look out for these symbols. The Law Of Attraction; Cosmic Media LLC. https://thelawofattraction.com/angel-signs-symbols/

JABAMIAH. (n.d.). Symbolikon - Visual Library of Worldwide Ancient Symbols. https://symbolikon.com/downloads/jabamiah-angel/

KatrinaKoltes. (2020, October 15). Ask The Angels - Angelic Sigils and Keys. Katrina Koltes. https://katrinakoltes.com/ask-the-angels-angelic-sigils-and-keys/

Kelly, A. (2021, December 24). A guide to angel numbers and what they mean. Allure. https://www.allure.com/story/what-are-angel-numbers

Kirsten, C. (2022, May 16). Who invented angel numbers? The truth behind numerology origins! Typically, Topical. https://typicallytopical.com/who-invented-angel-numbers/

Kurt. (2017, July 4). Finding your centre: Grounding meditation techniques. Earthing Canada. https://earthingcanada.ca/blog/grounding-meditation-techniques/

Law of Attraction visualization. (2022, October 13). Selfpause. https://selfpause.com/law-of-attraction/law-of-attraction-visualization-how-to-activate-the-law-of-attraction-through-visualization/

Lou. (2022, May 13). 9 common angel symbols and signs from your angels. A Little Spark of Joy. https://www.alittlesparkofjoy.com/angel-symbols/

Louise, E. (2020, February 14). Synchronicity and signs from the Universe that you shouldn't ignore. Through the Phases. https://www.throughthephases.com/synchronicity-signs-from-universe/

Marissa. (2021, January 1). 10 powerful vision board ideas to master the law of attraction. A to Zen Life. https://atozenlife.com/vision-board-ideas/

Meaningful coincidences, serendipity, and synchronicity. (n.d.). Psychology Today. https://www.psychologytoday.com/intl/blog/connecting-coincidence/202101/meaningful-coincidences-serendipity-and-synchronicity

Miedaner, T. (2015, February 25). 3 laws of Attraction: Like Attracts Like, Nature Abhors a Vacuum, The Present is Always Perfect. Lifecoach.com. https://www.lifecoach.com/articles/laws-of-attraction/3-laws-attraction-the-present-is-always-perfect/

Moore, J. D. (2016, July 24). 7 shocking ways angels speak to you every day. Psych Central. https://psychcentral.com/blog/life-goals/2016/07/ways-angels-speak-to-you

Moore, J. D. (2016, July 24). 7 shocking ways angels speak to you every day. Psych Central. https://psychcentral.com/blog/life-goals/2016/07/ways-angels-speak-to-you

O., T. (2021, October 15). Mirror hours: what are they trying to tell you? WeMystic. https://www.wemystic.com/mirror-hours/

Parlak, M. (2022, December 25). Deep spiritual meaning of mirrored numbers. Gemset. https://gemset.net/deep-spiritual-meaning-of-mirrored-numbers/

Paxton, P. (2022, February 15). Law of Attraction: History and overview - mind altar - medium. Mind Altar. https://medium.com/mind-altar/law-of-attraction-history-a-80bc52daa925

Powers, S., Barkataki, S., & Marglin, A. T. to. (2021, June 15). Everything you need to know about the solar plexus (navel) chakra. Yoga Journal. https://www.yogajournal.com/yoga-101/chakras-yoga-for-beginners/intro-third-navel-chakra/

Quinn, J. (2023, January 10). What do angel numbers mean, and why do you see them everywhere? Reader's Digest. https://www.rd.com/article/angel-numbers-meaning/

Rebecca Joy Stanborough, M. F. A. (2020, November 13). What is vibrational energy? Healthline. https://www.healthline.com/health/vibrational-energy

San, D., & Ph, F. D. (n.d.). Angels As Spiritual Guides. Digitalcommons.nl.edu. https://digitalcommons.nl.edu/cgi/viewcontent.cgi?article=1054&context=faculty_publications#:~:text=These%20spiritual%20beings%20are%20thought,different%20times%20in%20their%20life.

Sappington, T. (2020, September 10). The spirit world: Angels. The Gospel Coalition. https://www.thegospelcoalition.org/essay/the-spirit-world-angels/

Scott, E. (2007, February 18). What is the law of attraction? Verywell Mind. https://www.verywellmind.com/understanding-and-using-the-law-of-attraction-3144808

Sendef, G. (2016, September 26). 5 common ways angels bring you guidance and messages. Change Your Thoughts; Steven Aitchison. https://www.stevenaitchison.co.uk/5-common-ways-angels-bring-guidance-messages/

Siegel, J. (2022, May 4). Your angel number: What it means and how to discover it. WikiHow. https://www.wikihow.com/Find-My-Angel-Number

Sipress, J. (2021, July 21). Everything you need to know about angel numbers. Cosmopolitan. https://www.cosmopolitan.com/lifestyle/a37079416/angel-numbers-numerology/

Spiegelhalter, D. (2012, April 26). Coincidences: What are the chances of them happening? BBC. https://www.bbc.com/future/article/20120426-what-a-coincidence

Stokes, V. (2021, May 6). How to open your third eye chakra for spiritual awakening. Healthline. https://www.healthline.com/health/mind-body/how-to-open-your-third-eye

Tamara. (2022, October 29). 7 beautiful angel signs and symbols of love and support. Tamara Like Camera; Tamara. https://tamaracamerablog.com/7-beautiful-angel-signs-and-symbols-of-love-and-support/

Taphorn, S., & Taphorn, S. (n.d.). 5 warning signs from the angels. Beliefnet.com. https://www.beliefnet.com/inspiration/angels/5-warning-signs-from-the-angels.aspx

The law of attraction, simplified: A primer on this spiritual concept. (2020, April 24). Mindbodygreen. https://www.mindbodygreen.com/articles/the-law-of-attraction-simplified-what-it-is-and-how-to-use-it

Thorp, T. (2018, August 2). A meditation guide to activate the Law Of Attraction & love. Chopra. https://chopra.com/articles/a-meditation-guide-to-activate-the-law-of-attraction-love

Thorp, T. (2019, February 4). Guided meditation: Ground yourself using the Earth element. Chopra. https://chopra.com/articles/guided-meditation-ground-yourself-using-the-earth-element

Wang, C. (2022, September 5). The Sigil of Archangel Michael: What Is It and How to Use It? Buddha & Karma. https://buddhaandkarma.com/blogs/guide/what-is-the-sigil-of-archangel-michael-meaning

What is the Law of Attraction & how does it work? (2023, March 7). The Law Of Attraction; Cosmic Media LLC. https://thelawofattraction.com/what-is-the-law-of-attraction/

White, L., & White, L. (n.d.). 7 common ways angels bring you guidance and messages. Beliefnet.com. https://www.beliefnet.com/inspiration/angels/galleries/7-common-ways-angels-bring-you-guidance-and-messages.aspx

Why certain numbers keep showing up in your life + what to do when you see them. (2017, May 26). Mindbodygreen. https://www.mindbodygreen.com/articles/angel-number-sequences-and-what-they-mean-for-you

Wille. (2021, December 28). Angel number 7777 - A call for spirituality and meditation. A Little Spark of Joy. https://www.alittlesparkofjoy.com/angel-number-7777/

Wille. (2022, January 18). What are angel colors and what do they mean? A Little Spark of Joy. https://www.alittlesparkofjoy.com/angel-colors/

Young, A. (2019, November 7). Learn numerology: An easy-to-understand beginners guide. Subconscious Servant. https://subconsciousservant.com/learn-numerology

Made in the USA
Columbia, SC
30 May 2024

36342636R00065